THE DOW JONES-IRWIN GUIDE TO ESTATE PLANNING

William C. Clay, Jr.

THE DOW JONES-IRWIN GUIDE TO ESTATE PLANNING

FIFTH EDITION

DOW JONES-IRWIN Homewood, Illinois 60430

This publication is designed to provide accurate and
authoritative information in regard to the subject matter
covered. It is sold with the understanding that the
publisher is not engaged in rendering legal, accounting, or
other professional service. If legal advice or other expert
assistance is required, the services of a competent
professional person should be sought.

*From a Declaration of Principles jointly adopted by a Committee
of the American Bar Association and a Committee of Publishers.*

ISBN 0-87094-361-8
Library of Congress Catalog Card No. 82-72367

Printed in the United States of America

1 2 3 4 5 6 7 8 9 0 K 0 9 8 7 6 5 4 3 2

PREFACE

This book is about the objectives of estate planning. You might prefer to have a treatise on how to write your own will, but that would be no more practical than one on how to remove your own tonsils. You cannot do your estate planning alone, but this book will help you to identify an expert and, by being well informed yourself, to get the most out of his or her talents.

This book answers three questions: Why should you create an estate plan? What kind of an estate plan should you choose? When should you review and revise your estate plan? This book is emphatically not a do-it-yourself guide to either the design or the drafting of an estate plan. It is only a *why, what,* and *when* discussion of the basics of estate planning. This book deals with what you as a layman need to know.

Estate planning is a family affair. In a marriage, no matter who owns the property already acquired, the couple should share the opportunity and the challenge of developing together a better plan for the management, enjoyment, and disposition of what they own and of all that they hope to accumulate in the future. Furthermore, in most states, a surviving spouse has a right to renounce a will and to claim a statutory share of the estate. This can have a damaging, if not a disastrous, consequence upon an estate plan. This option should be openly discussed, and if there is a serious possibility of its being exercised, the estate should be planned accordingly.

From the point of view of planning, it is usually wiser for the husband and wife to keep their own estates separate and apart. This has an added advantage if, unfortunately, the marriage should ultimately be dissolved.

But couples should plan their estates together. This is not the only way a marriage should work, but upon the death of either party, the survivor should not have to conduct a search to discover what is owned and what should be done with it. Estate planning is an opportunity to share information and ambitions and to develop together hopes and expectations for the future.

Although the primary emphasis of this book is on the family, those who are single as well as those who are married should plan their estates.

Each of our 50 states has its own laws relating to the division of property when a person dies without a will. There are wide disparities, too, in state inheritance and estate tax laws and also in statutes relating to the administration of estates. A four- or five-volume treatise would be required to cover the idiosyncracies of estate planning in each of the 50 jurisdictions. Necessarily, the treatment here is general, but it does cover the basic principles in estate planning in the common law states and also in nine community property jurisdictions: Arizona, California, Idaho, Louisiana, New Mexico, Nevada, Puerto Rico, Texas, and Washington.

I hope you will discover that you need a will, a living will, and a power of attorney. Estate planning embraces the drafting of these documents but far more. Some of the objectives are (1) to create security during working and retiring years, (2) to provide support at death for spouse and children, (3) to minimize federal estate taxes and state inheritance taxes, (4) to design a program of gifts, (5) to reduce income taxes, (6) to ensure equitable (not necessarily equal) treatment for children, (7) to maintain a family business or farm intact, (8) to design a life insurance program, (9) to designate pension and profit-sharing beneficiaries, (10) to organize a business enterprise, (11) to review health and casualty insurance coverages, and (12) to provide for the custody of minor children.

A final caveat: Tax laws are constantly changing. What is true today might not be true tomorrow. The relevance of that observation is apparent from the fact that the Tax Reform Act of 1976 prompted the publication of a revised edition in January of 1977;

the Revenue Act of 1978 made it necessary to offer a third edition; additional amendments to the Internal Revenue Code, regulations, and decisions compelled the publication of a fourth edition; and now the Economic Recovery Tax Act of 1981 necessitates this fifth revision which focuses upon estate planning after January 1, 1982.

This book is only what it purports to be: a layman's guide to estate planning. You must, above all, employ well-qualified legal counsel. Then and only then will your estate planning accurately reflect your needs in the light of existing tax laws.

William C. Clay, Jr.

CONTENTS

chapter 1

WHY YOU NEED AN ESTATE PLAN

Estate planning is the art of designing a program for the effective management, enjoyment, and disposition of property at the least possible tax cost. Tax savings should never be the primary objective, but you should plan your estate so that you, your family, and others for whom you care receive the greatest possible beneficial enjoyment of what you own. You can achieve that goal and, at the same time, minimize taxes.

Whether you are rich or poor, single or married, parent or child, male or female, you need an estate plan. In one case a man died owning only meager personal possessions and a dilapidated house and lot worth no more than $3,500. A carelessly drawn will left his entire estate to his divorced daughter for life with remainder (ownership after life tenant dies) to her seven minor children, all of whom lived 700 miles away. No one was authorized to sell the property and reinvest the proceeds. The vacant, uninsured dwelling deteriorated day by day. The cost of qualifying a guardian for each child, instituting an action for a court sale, and reinvestment and managing and accounting for the proceeds overshadowed the value of the property. A simple will leaving the entire estate to the daughter would have been a better estate plan.

In another case, a wealthy woman without children died leaving her entire estate to her husband. A few months later, he died without a will, and his estate was divided among his nonresident nephews and nieces for whom neither he nor his wife cared. With an adequate estate plan, the wife by will could have left one half of her estate in trust for her husband, with that half after his death being added to a second trust created under the will for her nephews and nieces who had been solicitous and kind. Her husband could have also received the income from the second trust. Taxes would have been less, and the property would have been distributed to those for whom she cared.

Again, an unmarried college graduate with accumulated savings of $20,000 died in an accident, her parents and a sister surviving her. Both her mother and her father were financially secure, but they inherited her estate, and of course, it would be taxed again when it was passed on by them to their surviving daughter. A simple will leaving everything to her sister would have been far better estate planning.

As another example of a case involving no will, a farmer purchased a small, adjacent tract of land, taking title in the name of himself and his wife as tenants in common (each owning one half) without right of survivorship (survivor takes all). By a prior marriage she had had four children. Late in life the farmer, then a widower, wanted to sell the small, adjacent tract of land, but his wife's children by her first marriage would not agree. Preferably, of course, he should have taken title to the small tract either in his own name or as a joint tenant with his wife with right of survivorship.

A man with three minor children died without a will leaving an estate consisting principally of his home, which was encumbered by a mortgage. Under the laws of the state in which he lived, title to one half of the home vested in his widow and the other half in his three minor children. The family could not afford to retain the residence, and yet enormous expense was incurred through the necessity of guardianships for the children plus the cost of a judicially approved sale. A simple will leaving the entire estate to the wife would have eliminated all of that trouble and expense.

In yet another case, a husband and a wife died in an automobile accident, leaving two minor children to survive them. Although their combined estates were adequate for the support of the children, neither left a will and neither had ever negotiated a contract with a member of the family or with a friend for custody of the children. An intrafamily custody dispute developed, and the children were penalized further by the excessive court cost of guardianships. A will placing the estates in trust for the children and a custody contract would have constituted a more sensible estate plan.

Regrettably, for a variety of reasons, very few estates are planned, and in every county in the United States, court records reveal the tragic consequences. First, most of us are so concerned with living that we do not give any thought to the consequences of dying. Second, there has never been a widely read layman's guide to estate planning that explains the broad need for assistance in planning and outlines some of the basic techniques. Last, there are simply not enough lawyers who are well trained in estate planning and who are compassionate enough to care about even the smallest estates.

Other attorneys have reported the disastrous consequences of dying intestate. Jacob Fisher, a member of the New York Bar, in writing of *Human Drama in Death & Taxes,* tells the story of Freddy Towers who owned the best apartment house in town. With time to spare, he would drive his elderly tenants to any place where one of them wished to go. He was especially fond of the Brush family: a widow, her daughter Lucy, and a brother Bob who had lost a leg in an industrial accident. Inevitably, Freddy and Lucy were married. His attorney insisted that he have a will, but Freddy knew that under the laws of his state his wife, who was 10 years younger, would get everything. The attorney pointed out that Lucy might die before Freddy.

Tragically, while Freddy was driving an elderly tenant to her dentist, a young man stoned on drugs ran through a red light and crashed into the side of Freddy's car, killing him instantly. Overcome by grief, Freddy's widow died in the ambulance taking her to the hospital. Meanwhile, that state had adopted the Uniform Probate Code which provides that any person who fails to survive the decedent by 120 hours is presumed to have died before the decedent.

Freddy's estate went to two cousins in Florida whom he had never seen and never heard from. He would have preferred that his estate go to Lucy's elderly mother and to her crippled brother. Regrettably, he assumed that the laws of the state would make an adequate will for him.

Mr. Fisher also tells the story of Philip Kohler, a nine-year-old orphan, who was placed in a foster home with Louis and Martha Detweiler who had a daughter the same age. When they were teenagers, they fell in love and, being unrelated, were married.

Years later, Philip purchased an apartment-motel complex, taking title with himself and his wife as joint tenants with right of survivorship.

When Philip's foster father died, he left a lonely and desolate widow. Philip and his wife, Beatrice, persuaded Martha to move in with them, explaining that "our home is your home just like your home was our home. You will really be helping us out because we will have a chance to get out and have some fun once in a while."

During the winter months, the apartment-motel complex was closed, and the three lived in Florida.

One year in late December en route to Florida, Philip's car skidded on an icy road crashing headlong into a tree. His wife was dead when the first aid squad arrived. Philip was alive but unconscious. He died three days later. His foster mother, who had been sleeping in the back seat, received only a few minor bruises. Not only the apartment-motel complex but bank accounts were held by Philip and his wife jointly with right of survivorship. Because he outlived his wife, blood relatives, like worms coming out of the ground after a spring rain, claimed the entire estate, although Philip had never known of the relatives who had, of course, never assumed their responsibility of raising him as an orphan. His beloved mother-in-law was left penniless. If Philip had had a will, this story would have had a happy ending.

This book is emphatically not a do-it-yourself estate planning guide. Books on how to write your own will, how to avoid probate, and other comparable manuals have created more problems than they have solved. Estate planning is an art and a science beyond the mastery of any layman.

But this book can help you and your lawyer plan your estate. First, you will discover the importance of doing something now. Second, by understanding some of the basic techniques of estate planning, you can not only take the facts that an attorney will need to your first conference with him but you will save him the time of having to explain to you the principles that can be mastered by a close study of this book. You can help build for yourself a far better estate plan at a much lower cost. Finally, you will discover when your estate plan must be changed. You will not let yours get out of date.

chapter 2

MAKE A WILL

A will is the basic document of almost every estate plan. It is an instrument executed in the manner prescribed by statute whereby a person disposes of his property after his death. Ordinarily, a simple will contains only three primary provisions. First, an executor is nominated or appointed to carry out the provisions of the will. Second, the powers of the executor are defined. And, third, the will states the person or persons who are to receive your property after all the debts, funeral expenses, taxes, and costs of administration have been paid.

If you are an older male with a very small estate, an adequate will might consist of only the following words: "I leave all of my property to my wife, request that she be appointed executrix without bond, and authorize her to do everything that I could do with my property if living." Those few words in your own handwriting, followed by the date of execution and your signature would constitute what is called a holographic will, that is, one entirely in your own handwriting. In 19 states, a holographic will may be admitted to probate, the judicial process of establishing the validity of a will.

A simple will like that seldom suffices. For example, it does not provide for the disposition of property if your wife should die before you. Second, your wife at the time of your death may be ill or otherwise unable to serve as executrix. Nevertheless, simplicity sometimes works. Former President Calvin Coolidge's will said only: "I leave my entire estate to my wife, Grace, and request that she be appointed executrix without bond."

Ordinarily, however, an adequate estate plan embraces a typed will which is far more comprehensive and which is executed in the presence of two or three witnesses who must see both the maker of the will and each other sign the instrument. Two carefully drafted wills appear in Appendixes A and C, but high standards of draftmanship are not enough. Forms are suggestive and helpful, but no one can prepare a suitable will by selecting paragraphs from a form book. Every will must be molded to meet the situation it is designed to cover. A few illustrations may aid you in developing an approach.

First, you must understand that your net taxable estate will consist at least of (1) all of the property that you own in your own name at its value on the date of your death, (2) all or some part of the property that you own with your spouse as a joint tenant with right of survivorship, (3) life insurance proceeds, (4) pension and profit-sharing benefits payable to your estate, and (5) certain other assets, *less* (*a*) debts, (*b*) funeral expenses, and (*c*) costs of administering and settling your estate. Later in this book, you will have a chance to consider some of the advantages and disadvantages of joint ownerships and the many alternatives available under profit-sharing and pension plans. For the present, we shall stick strictly to the basics.

First, you should select an executor and one or more successor executors. The ideal executor (and you may never be able to find him) will possess excellent business judgment, be a paragon of honor and integrity, have experience in estate settlement, and have a vital and continuing concern for the care, comfort, and happiness of your family.

Second, you may wish for your will to declare that all the furniture and furnishings in your house belong to your wife. She probably thinks they do anyhow, and a recital of that fact may remove them from taxation in your estate. But you will have, of course, some tangible (touchable) personal property of your own which you would not want to have sold but would prefer to give either to your wife or to someone else. Personal letters, jewelry, automobiles, personal effects, clothing, and sporting equipment are typical examples of this kind of personal property.

Third, life insurance and profit-sharing and pension benefits are not disposed of by will but by a separate beneficiary designation. In those states which impose inheritance taxes, life insurance is occasionally exempt from the tax if payable to a designated beneficiary, which may include a trustee under a living trust (discussed in Chapter 3) or a trust under your will (discussed later in this chapter). Depending upon your situation, you may want to avoid the state inheritance tax or you may prefer to have insurance proceeds in your estate to pay debts and taxes. Unless payable in a lump sum, profit-sharing, Keogh Plan, and Individual Retirement Account benefits generally are not subject to the federal estate tax if payable to a designated beneficiary, and here again, you have a similar choice.

With these preliminaries out of the way, you must now make a choice about the distribution of the bulk of your estate. Here, for the first time, taxes become a major consideration. The cost of dying may be a pittance or a fortune. To a great extent, the price depends on how your estate is planned. Under the Economic Recovery Tax Act of 1981, in a net estate of $450,000, the U.S. death taxes in 1982 could be either $76,000 (without using the most advantageous marital deduction) or $0.00 (using a marital deduction of one half of the adjusted gross estate).

At one time, you could reduce your death taxes primarily by writing a will in which your wife was given either a legal or a trust estate for life in practically all of your estate with whatever might be left over at her death going to your children or other members of your family. This technique took advantage of the principle that as long as your property continued to pass under your will, death taxes would be assessed only at your death and not again at the death of your wife. Today, whenever a husband and wife have estates of approximately equal value, the best estate plan often is for each one to set up a life estate for the other with remainder going to the children. Here, however, it is assumed that your estate is much larger than your wife's, and in your case, a marital deduction will (discussed in this chapter) may be the best estate planning approach.

The basic idea of the marital deduction will is that you can now leave the greater of (a) all, or (b) any part of your adjusted gross estate (total taxable estate less debts, funeral expenses, and costs of administration) to your wife and that portion will be free from U.S. estate taxes at your death. That definition has more holes in it than a five-pound slab of Swiss cheese. Nevertheless, the fundamental theory is there. If you leave one half of your adjusted gross estate to your wife, that portion escapes tax until your wife dies. For 1982, each of you will have the equivalent of an exemption of $225,000. This increases annually until each of you is entitled to a $600,000 exemption equivalent in 1987. Then, too, because estate tax rates, like income tax rates, climb as more money is involved, when your estate is divided into two units, each unit is subject to a lower tax rate than would otherwise apply.

Incidentally, using the alternative marital deduction of leaving more than one half of your adjusted gross estate to your husband or wife could result in a higher tax being imposed. If the entirety of an estate is left to a husband or to a wife, the tax would admittedly be less when the first one dies. Later, however, at the death of the survivor, the tax assessed would be substantially larger by avoidance of all tax upon the death of the first of the couple to die. This is illustrated in Appendix F. For example, assume that the husband dies in 1987 with an adjusted gross estate of $1.2 million and that the wife does not have an individual estate of her own. If the entire estate is left to her, there would be no federal tax upon the death of the husband, but assuming the estate remains at the same size, the tax upon the death of the wife would be $235,000. Someone has facetiously called this the "Reagan Tax Trap."

There are a number of ways of writing a marital deduction will. First, the deductible portion can be left outright to your wife. Second, as an alternative, you may create an estate trust, or a power of appointment trust may be established. Third, and this is a viable alternative, the wife may be left a life estate with remainder to children upon the death of the wife. In a law school textbook, each of these three approaches would be described in detail and their relative advantages and disadvantages measured. Here, however, we will simply attempt to give you enough information so that you may, with your lawyer, decide what you should do. In all probability, you would choose a typical power of appointment trust, placing in it only one half of your adjusted gross estate. Here is how that would work.

First, in your will, you nominate not only an executor but a trustee, who will probably be the same person, to manage your estate during the life of your wife. Two trusts of approximately equal value will be created. Let's call the first of these the "Wife's Trust," and the other we shall identify as the "Family Trust." You will direct the trustee to pay out of the wife's trust all of the income to your wife for life and also to pay her as much of the principal as she may need to maintain the standard of living to which she is accustomed. At her death, your trustee will be directed to distribute any balance remaining in this trust exactly as your wife tells him by deed or will to distribute it. This action on her part is called the exercise of a power of appointment. If your wife does not exercise the power of appointment, however, you will direct your trustee to distribute the balance of the wife's trust over into the family trust.

Your marital deduction trust will not only save taxes but it will also give your wife an added measure of security and a valuable discretionary power. Because she has the right to decide how one half of your estate shall be distributed at her death, the odds are that she will get greater interest and attention from your children. Somehow, a potential inheritance or loss of inheritance seems to strengthen love. Second, your wife's right to distribute the principal of her trust is a valuable power in emergencies. For example, by illness or accident, one of your children may become unable to support himself. Then, too, moral equality, rather than mathematical equality, may become an objective and your wife may wish to distribute a greater part of her trust to her disabled child.

You may also wish to direct your trustee, if the wife's trust assets are exhausted, to pay as much of the income and principal of the family trust to your wife as she may need to maintain her standard of living. Next, your trustee may be authorized, but not required, to distribute out of the family trust income and principal sufficient for the education, maintenance, and support of each of your children after considering other sources of income and support which each may have from time to time. After your wife's death, your trustee may be authorized to distribute all of the assets of your estate among your children at such time or times and in such amounts as he may in his discretion determine. Alternatively, of course, you may require your trustee to distribute your estate to your children upon the death of your wife or upon their having reached a certain age.

Essentially, a marital deduction will such as we have been talking about makes your entire estate available to your wife as she needs it and lets the rest go to your children at the least possible tax cost.

Please do not leap to the conclusion that you should have a marital deduction will. It is impossible to design one approach which will give the perfect answer to any given estate-planning problem. Each estate is unique. Any particular program is dependent upon the comparative size of your estate and your wife's estate, methods of disposition, kinds of property involved, impact of both federal and state

chapter 3

CREATE A TRUST

If you will add up what you own, what you expect to get by inheritance or otherwise from others, insurance proceeds, and other assets, you may discover to your surprise that you are worth more than you ever dreamed. If the total should exceed the exemption equivalent shown at the end of Appendix E, you should consider a marital deduction will. But for a variety of reasons you may wish to reject that approach.

First, if you are unwilling to give your wife the power to appoint by her will one half of your taxable estate, then consider using a marital deduction will leaving a life estate to your wife with remainder to your children. For example, if your wife has had children by a prior marriage for whom you do not care, then you had better think twice before giving her a power to make provision for them. She could also, of course, give that part of your estate over which she has some control to a man whom she might marry after your death. But generally speaking, if you have children only by your marriage, the odds are that she will permit her trust to pour over into theirs.

Secondly, if your wife has a large estate of her own, you had better ask your attorney to plan the two estates together. Quite often in that situation, a marital deduction provision will increase rather than reduce death taxes. You may wish to use a portion but

11

not all of the available marital deduction. For example, you could leave your wife one third rather than one half of your adjusted gross estate or alternatively, if you trust her, authorize her to disclaim (not take) a portion of her trust.

Finally, if you are the wife rather than the husband and if you have a large estate of your own, you may assume that your husband will remarry upon your death, and you may have not the slightest interest in exposing your estate to the risk that your husband might use part of it upon a second wife. You may wish to give your husband only a life estate which will qualify for the marital deduction with remainder to your children.

If a husband plans to leave his estate in fee simple (outright) to his wife or to his adult children or to other persons free from disability or to charities, a simple will may suffice. If, however, he wants to give someone the use and benefit of his estate for life with his properties to be divided among others thereafter, then he should consider creating a trust.

The duties of an executor are limited and temporary in character. Generally speaking, he takes possession of personal property, pays debts, funeral expenses, costs of administration, and death taxes and then distributes the estate in the manner provided by the will. Trust management begins where estate settlement ends. Generally, the same person that is appointed as executor is also appointed as trustee, which has some distinct advantages from the standpoints of both administration and taxation. Early distributions from an executor to a trustee are safer for the executor if he is also the trustee because he can always get a pay-back from the trust if the needs of the estate require that, and furthermore, income taxes can often be saved during administration by using a trust as a separate taxpayer.

A trust under a will is created by leaving properties to a named trustee for management with income and principal to be distributed by the trustee according to directions contained in the will. More than one trust can be created under a will, and a separate trustee can be named for each trust. For example, you could appoint each of your adult children as trustee of his or her own trust.

Some of the most unsatisfactory wills ever written have left property to someone for life with the remainder to someone else. This is called a legal life estate because title is in the life tenant for life rather than in a trustee. For example, if you should create a legal life in a farm in favor of your wife with remainder to your children, all kinds of problems could arise. Would your wife have to insure buildings? If one of them burned down, would she have to replace it to the extent of insurance proceeds or would she have to supplement those with her own money to restore a building of like size and quality? Who would receive crops planted but not harvested in the year of the life tenant's death? Who, if anyone, could sell the farm and reinvest the proceeds? What would be done with monies received from the condemnation of a part of the land for the construction of a highway or pipeline? How should taxes be prorated in the year of the life tenant's death?

Problems become more complex if an effort is made to create a legal life estate in personal property. Fixtures and equipment wear out and have to be replaced. Livestock either dies or matures and must be sold. The most carefully drawn will may create or leave unsolved countless questions concerning a life tenant's right to use or dispose of property and concerning division of income. Admittedly, a legal life estate can be created and some of these problems met, but for the most part, it is far easier and wiser to create a trust.

If you have two or more children, you may wish to create a family trust divided into as many equal shares as you have children with each share being known as a child's trust. You can direct your trustee, charging an equal portion to each child's trust, to pay your wife that part of the income and principal thereof necessary to provide for her according to the standard of living that she is enjoying at the date of your death and to enable her to provide as she wishes for your children. You may wish to let your wife's benefits end if she should remarry. Instead, it might be wiser to direct your trustee, in making distributions to your wife, to take into consideration all other sources of income and support which she might have from time to time. For example, if you should die leaving minor children, both your wife and your children might be better off it she should remarry. Admittedly, you would not want to support her second husband, but if he too should die or should become disabled, surely you would not want your wife starving while your trustee continued to support your children.

Next in your will, you can authorize the trustee to accumulate income to the extent that the laws of your state permit or to distribute to your children any income not paid to your wife. You may also authorize your trustee to pay expenses directly for the maintenance and education of your children out of either income or principal.

Preferably, payments to your children should be charged equally to each child's trust until all of your children have reached an age of somewhere between 23 and 28 years. After all, if you should die after one child had completed college but before another one had entered college, it would hardly be fair to divide your estate equally among your children until all of them had first received comparable benefits from your estate.

After a particular child has reached the age level selected by you, then you may wish to authorize your trustee to supplement that child's earnings for his or her maintenance or support, provided, of course, that the trustee must first be sure to hold back enough principal for the protection of your wife and younger children. You may even want to give the trustee the power to purchase a home for a child, keeping title in the name of the trust or placing title in the name of the child. The trustee may also be authorized to make loans to the child with or without security, and if you prefer, you make this or any other power contingent upon your trustee obtaining advance approval of your wife.

You may, upon the death of your wife and after all of your children have reached the age level selected by you, give the trustee the power to make partial and final distributions to your children whenever the trustee believes it to be in the best interest of the child. For example, if you have a son or daughter whose marriage is insecure or is unable to manage property, your trustee may find it wise to keep that child's share in trust for a period of time and, perhaps, even throughout his or her life. Now, you cannot foresee the future. Later, after your children have matured, you may prefer to revise your will, making your own decision as to which shares should be paid outright and which should be kept in trust.

If you plan to will any income-producing properties to minor children, a trust is a virtual imperative. Without it, a guardian would have to qualify for each child, giving bond (guaranty with surety) to secure performance of his duties. Second, in most states, the guardian could invest only in land, government bonds, and other legals (a class of securities in which trustees may legally invest). In many states, a guardian would not have the right to purchase livestock to place upon a farm. Third, the guardian could not use up the principal even for the purpose of educating a minor without the approval of the court, and, of course, without judicial approval, he could not enter into a mortgage or long-term lease. Finally, he would have to file a settlement with the court periodically. Statutes do not grant guardians the powers that can be conferred upon trustees by will, and consequently a guardian cannot be expected to earn as much for his ward as a trustee nor to have comparable freedom in taking care of the needs of minor children.

Worst of all, if you leave any income-producing assets to the child, when he or she comes of age (at 18 or 21), the child will take over the management of the assets for himself. There are very few children of that age who are capable of managing their own financial affairs. All too often, there is a temptation for an early marriage, an expensive sports car, a costly trip, or a half-baked business venture.

A trust is one of the most versatile and useful of all estate planning devices: Taxes are minimized, minors are better protected, and property management is simplified and improved.

chapter 4

CONSIDER A LIVING TRUST

Trusts are the most versatile methods known for disposing of property, but so far, we have considered only trusts created by a will. Two basic varieties of these have been considered: (1) A wife's trust and a family trust using the marital deduction and (2) a family trust under which someone, usually a surviving wife, is given lifetime benefits with division to be made thereafter to others, usually children. These two varieties and many other kinds of trusts can also be created during your lifetime. They are known as "living" or "*inter vivos*" trusts. A living trust can be drafted so that you can amend it (change it) or revoke it (call the whole deal off) at any time. Alternately, a living trust can be made irrevocable (not subject to any change whatsoever).

During recent years, the revocable living trust, which is what this chapter is about, has had great publicity and become very popular. First, an excellent film was released by the American Bar Association: *The Revocable Trust—An Essential Tool for the Practicing Lawyer.* Second, Norman F. Dacey's *How to Avoid Probate* advocated a living trust as the answer to every problem in estate planning, which is about as sensible as contending that a suit of clothes can be manufactured which will fit every man, no matter what his height or weight. Actually, in many cases, its use is wise and intelligent, and in many, many others, it has little, if any, value whatsoever.

To create a living trust, all that you have to do is transfer property by an agreement to a trustee to be held by the trustee for the use of the beneficiaries in the way prescribed by the agreement. In the living trust, you can either use a marital deduction agreement or set up a single family trust, for example, for your wife and children. If the trust is revocable, the property in the trust will continue to be a part of your estate for death tax purposes. Therefore, tax savings are seldom the motivation for creating a living trust.

If you have a large portfolio of life insurance, the creation of a living trust may be the best foundation for your estate plan. In many states, life insurance payable to a named beneficiary, including a trustee under a living trust, is exempt from state death taxes. For two reasons, you are better off having your insurance made payable to the trustee of a living trust. First, the proceeds can be made available through the trust to your executor for the payment of debts, funeral expenses, costs of administration, and death taxes. This arrangement can be advantageous because insurance proceeds are often needed to avoid the forced sale of land, a closely held business, a home, or some other fixed asset to obtain funds to cover estate obligations.

Second, if your life insurance is made payable to your wife, it may be exempt from state death taxes when you die, but upon her death, any unexpected portions of these funds will be a part of her estate subject to taxation. Also, your trustee may be better qualified to invest and manage life insurance proceeds than either your wife or your children. In fact, if you have minor children, a guardian would have to qualify for each, and a trusteeship is far more efficient than a guardianship.

Furthermore, if you die before retirement and if either your estate or a named beneficiary becomes entitled to pension, profit-sharing, Keogh, or individual retirement account benefits, you should by all means consider the creation of a living trust. Whenever qualified retirement benefits (other than lump-sum benefits) are payable to a named beneficiary, including the trustee of a living trust, these are totally exempt from the federal estate tax.

There is a third situation in which a living trust is by far the best estate-planning technique. If you are an elderly person with a large estate, you can create a living trust naming, for example, one or more of your children as trustees. By placing substantially all of your property in the trust, you will be relieved of the worries of managing your property, and, if your trustee does not perform to your expectations, you can always revoke the trust.

In the fourth place, the living trust is the ideal solution for a problem that is becoming ever increasingly common. If you live in one state and your children reside in another, they may not be eligible to qualify as executors and trustees under your will. Usually, too, a trust should be administered in the state where your beneficiaries reside. This problem can easily be solved by putting all, or substantially all, of your property in a living trust, naming as trustee either your children or a bank, for example, in the community where your children live.

Finally, a living trust avoids the delays of probate and publicity about the size of your estate and the names of your beneficiaries. If you treasure the right of privacy, a living trust is the ideal vehicle for avoiding publication of the size and disposition of your estate.

A trust, of course, does not come into existence until it has been funded, that is, until some asset has been transferred to the trustee. Life insurance is only one of the many things which can be used to fund the trust. Cash, securities, real estate, or any other asset may be used.

If you create a living trust as part of your estate plan, you will also in all probability want to have a will leaving all of your residuary estate to the trustee of your living trust so that the bulk of your remaining estate will "pour over" into and be administered as part of your living trust. A sample, and it is only a sample, of a living trust appears in Appendix B and of a pour-over will in Appendix C.

Contrary to popular belief, the use of a living trust seldom reduces significantly either attorney fees or fiduciary fees for services rendered in the settlement of an estate. The services of both counsel and trustee in the preparation of tax returns and the management and administration of assets are virtually the same whether your estate is disposed of by will or in part by the creation of a living trust. In some jurisdictions, however, legal and fiduciary fees are less when a living trust is used, and almost invariably, avoidance of judicial supervision eliminates bond premiums and court costs for the trusteeship.

chapter 5

GRANT POWERS OF APPOINTMENT

A power of appointment should never be created without the advice of an attorney who understands fully all of the tax and legal consequences. Powers improperly designed and used can seriously penalize you and your family. And yet, with competent advice, you not only can, but should, grant powers of appointment. There is no more valuable technique in estate planning.

Here, perhaps more than anywhere else, this book is not intended to be a do-it-yourself estate planning guide but only an explanation suggesting some of the alternatives available to you.

Powers of appointment are not simply a tax-saving device but primarily a means of disposing of your property more efficiently. Nevertheless, in most cases, you can accomplish your basic objective and at the same time save taxes. For that reason, we will begin by explaining what a power of appointment is and outline the tax aspects of powers of appointment in estate planning.

A power of appointment may be created by will, by deed, or by contract. The person who creates the power is called the donor, and the person to whom the power is given is known as the donee. The appointee is anyone in whose favor a donee exercises the power. The property interest covered by the power of appointment is sometimes called the appointed property.

In considering tax aspects, we shall, for the purpose of simplicity, deal only with powers to be created now, excluding, among others, those granted prior to October 22, 1942 when the Internal Revenue Code was amended. At the present time, a power is general if it can be exercised in favor of the donee or his estate or the creditors of either and if the donee can exercise it alone, that is, without someone else with a substantial adverse interest having to join in. A general power of appointment is taxable whether exercised or not. Most of the time, a wife is given a general power of appointment in the creation of a wife's trust to take advantage of the marital deduction.

Under a special power of appointment, on the other hand, the donee may appoint only from a limited class of persons other than himself, his estate, and his creditors. Ordinarily, a special power of appointment permits appointment only to designated members of the family, usually children, grandchildren, and in-laws. Whereas a general power of appointment is taxable whether exercised or not, under the federal law, a special power of appointment may be taxable only if it is exercised. State laws differ on the tax consequences of the exercise or nonexercise of special powers of appointment.

While a general power of appointment is used most frequently in the creation of a wife's trust to take advantage of the marital deduction, it has an additional value. A wife with a general power of appointment retains greater authority over her children, and she has the freedom to make unequal distributions to them. I shall never forget an estate in which a son, after the death of his father, ceased speaking to his mother and opened a business competing with the principal enterprise of his father's estate. He gave his mother every reason to use her power of appointment so that he would not receive additional benefits from that portion of his father's estate which had been placed in a trust for his mother. Repeatedly, too, I have seen examples of one of a number of children suffering a crippling disability, thus destroying his ability to support himself. In such a case, there is justification for a mother to use her power of appointment to provide for the health, support, and maintenance of her unfortunate child. Preferably, however, to avoid the inadvertent exercise of a general power of appointment, the donee, in exercising the power, should be required by deed or will to make specific reference to the instrument granting the power.

A special power of appointment, like a general power of appointment, is designed to permit the donee of the power to make adjustments in estate distribution which are needed because of events occurring after the creation of the power. For example, if you have minor children or minor grandchildren, you probably cannot, at the time the power is created, foresee their future needs. Nor is there any way for you to predict the ultimate outcome of the marriage of either a child or a grandchild. A special power of appointment enables someone else whom you trust to modify your estate plan to take care of changed conditions when they arise.

If you have a daughter, the creation of a power of appointment is especially desirable. First, you can direct your trustee to pay her income and principal necessary for the education, health, maintenance, and support of her and also of her children. If, instead, you should leave part of your estate to her in fee simple (outright), then if she should die before her husband, he could disclaim (refuse to accept) under any will which she might have and receive part of her estate by statute. Furthermore, if you are leaving a substantial estate to your daughter, she could save death taxes, perhaps, only by using the marital deduction, and neither you nor she might be interested in turning over one half of what you are giving her to her husband. On the other hand, you could give your daughter a special power of appointment which probably would not be taxable unless she exercised it. In default of the exercise, you could provide that the trust would continue for the benefit of her children, but you could confer upon her the right to make provision for her husband and to make an unequal distribution among her children.

In the creation of powers of appointment, income tax consequences must be considered. If a son is named as trustee, the income may be taxed to him and even where he is not named as trustee, he may be subject to a tax to the extent that income is used for the support of one of his children. Certain powers in living trusts will also result in the income being taxed to the person creating the trust.

Without adverse tax consequences, you can also grant a beneficiary a power to appoint to himself in any year, out of the principal of his trust, $5,000 or 5 percent of the principal of the trust. Then if the trustee is not sufficiently generous, the object of your affection can receive, in addition to income, a part of the principal every year.

You might also want to consider giving your trustee what might be called, in a broad sense, a power of appointment, that is, the power to provide for your children until they reach a designated age according to their needs rather than according to some standard of mathematical equality. This device is known as a sprinkling trust: The trustee may use the money where, in his opinion, it will do the most good.

Once again, using a power of appointment in its broadest sense, you may authorize your wife or one of your children to appoint a successor trustee. That procedure is particularly appropriate when at the time you are preparing your will it is impossible to foresee whether you would prefer a particular individual or a certain bank to act as trustee 20, 30, or 40 years later.

A well-designed estate plan should be not a straitjacket but a charter of freedom. By building in flexibility, you can not only save taxes but also make wiser provision for those you love.

chapter 6

PICK YOUR OWN FIDUCIARY

An administrator, an executor, and a trustee—all are fiduciaries (persons holding property in trust). If you die without a will, the court will appoint an administrator who may or may not be qualified to manage the personal property in your estate, but who will collect assets, pay debts, funeral expenses, and administrative expenses, and distribute the balance according to the law. Ordinarily, an administrator will not have any power to deal with the real estate, not even to the extent of managing a farm during the current crop year. An executor, by contrast, can be selected by you and empowered to deal not only with your personal estate but also with your real estate. Comparatively speaking, the assignment of an executor or of an administrator is of a short-term nature extending over a period of only one, two, of three years, whereas the functions of a trustee, whose services begin where those of an executor end, may extend over decades or even lifetimes.

The selection of an executor and, usually too, of a trustee is a challenging assignment of enormous importance. Ideally, the executor-trustee should have extensive fiduciary experience and demonstrated ability as a businessman. Integrity is vital, and of paramount importance too is a genuine and compassionate concern for the welfare of the beneficiaries of your estate. Choosing a well-qualified executor-trustee is often one of the most difficult problems in the planning of an estate.

You may be tempted to designate your spouse and to rely upon your attorney to guide the executor-trustee through the maze of responsibilities, including liquidation or operation of business, making elections under the Internal Revenue Code, preparing income and death tax returns, discovering postmortem estate-planning opportunities, and keeping the estate beneficiaries informed and happy. This may work, but there are sometimes better options available. A brother, sister, adult child or business associate is often a better choice, but a problem can arise if one of a number of children is selected to serve and especially so if the trustee is vested with discretionary powers in making distributions. He or she may be placed in an embarrassing and emotionally charged position of having to treat each brother and sister differently. Furthermore, by possessing powers to make distributions of principal to himself or to his children as beneficiaries, some income and death tax savings possibilities may be forfeited and lost. For example, if a son, while in office as trustee, can distribute principal to himself, that portion of the assets may be included in his estate when he dies, and if he uses estate funds to support his own children, he may lose the right to claim them as dependents on his own income tax return.

If an individual is appointed as executor-trustee, he may die before you do, and certainly there is a greater risk that he will die before the trust created by you terminates. The selection of a successor also becomes of vital importance. One useful alternative is to authorize a surviving spouse or one or more children to designate a successor executor, but that power may not be exercised, and someone must be designated to serve in the event of a default. In almost every will, the ultimate executor-trustee should be a bank with a well-organized and administered trust department. The bank will not die, and if you live in a metropolitan area, it should be possible to identify some institution with a good record in administration of estates and trusts.

Often, the best choice for an executor-trustee to serve from the beginning is a bank with an excellent trust department, but in smaller communities, there are not many of these and there is always a risk that the trust officer, in whom you have confidence, may die before an estate and trust settlement is complete.

Before selecting anyone other than a bank as executor-trustee, consider the many things that your fiduciary must do. Preferably, except in the most simple estates, a double-entry set of books should be opened, and if there is a marital and nonmarital trust which cannot be combined for administrative purposes, two sets of books must be opened. If any trust allows for accumulation of income, there must be a separate account showing all accumulations, which must be segregated until they are paid out. Records must be maintained so that income and ad valorem (at a rate percent of value) tax returns may be prepared and beneficiaries advised of the character (whether taxable or nontaxable) of distributions made to them. The position of the trustee, especially, is not one for an amateur.

Another possibility is that of naming of coexecutors and as cotrustees a spouse or a child and a bank with a trust department either with or without some clear-cut division of responsibility between the two. For example, a wife is in a better position to determine distributions to be made to children under a sprinkling trust, whereas ordinarily, a bank is better qualified to manage a portfolio of securities.

Eligibility to serve as executor can also be a problem. In most states, a nonresident child may serve although he may be required to designate a process agent and to give bond. Ordinarily, a bank not incorporated in the state where you live will not be eligible to qualify unless, as some states permit, a coexecutor-trustee qualified to do business in the state is also nominated to serve. If you are a resident of one state and also own property in another state, then you should ask your attorney to examine the requirements of the foreign jurisdiction. Sometimes an ancillary executor-trustee must be designated to serve in the foreign jurisdiction, but there are ways of getting around this. For example, if you own a summer home in another state, ancillary administration can be avoided by transferring the title to this home to the survivor of your wife and yourself with remainder to your children with a power being reserved in your wife and yourself as life tenants to sell and reinvest. Another possibility is to place property located in a foreign jurisdiction in a revocable trust.

Unless your will provides otherwise, an executor and also a trustee will be required to give bond to secure performance of his duties as such. Unless there is a member of your family or a friend who can be counted on to sign a bond without compensation, the cost of purchasing this protection from an insurance company can

chapter 7

EMPOWER YOUR
EXECUTOR-TRUSTEE
TO ACT

If you are engaged in business at the time of your death, in most states neither your executor nor your trustee can lawfully carry on your business without a specific authorization. If he takes his chances and operates it, he will be liable for any losses that may result.

By his will, the newspaper publisher Joseph Pulitzer imposed certain inflexible conditions which could not be complied with upon the sale of the *New York World.* After expensive litigation, the conditions were set aside, but when the *World* was sold, publication had to be suspended. Another publisher, Adolph S. Ochs, received better advice. He gave his executors and trustees broad powers of management and disposition of his interest in the *New York Times.*

A small-town druggist said nothing in his will about the operation of his store. Because the executor played it safe, the family suffered. The drugstore was gradually liquidated. When inventories of cigarettes, razor blades, and other repeat sale items were exhausted, they were not replaced. The business fizzled to a failure, whereas with an adequate power to the executor, it could have been sold profitably as a going concern with another drugstore paying a premium to purchase the prescription file. The same will, in lieu of devising realty to a trustee, left rental properties to the wife for life with remainder to nephews and nieces. The buildings deteriorated, approaching the end of their useful life, but an expensive suit had to be filed for authorization to sell and reinvest the proceeds.

Money can be earned and expenses curtailed by granting your executor and your trustee the power to do virtually anything that you could do with your property if you were living. You should select a fiduciary whom you can trust and give him all of the powers that he needs to act. In today's complex civilization, a simple one-page will seldom suffices. Neither the common law nor the statutes of your state confer upon your executor-trustee the powers which he should have.

Ordinarily, neither a will nor trust agreement needs to embrace all of the powers contained in the sample will (Appendix A) and in the sample trust agreement (Appendix B), but preferably each of them should contain at least the broad grant of powers which appears in Article III of the typical short will in Appendix D.

Second, if your estate is not well diversified in its investments, you may wish to authorize your executor-trustee to retain any property which you own as original investments although some might not be of the quality required under the laws of the state in which you live.

Next, if you own a business, it is imperative that your executor-trustee be authorized to operate and/or to dispose of that business.

During administration of your estate and during administration of any trust that you may create, your trustee should be given a broad power of investment and reinvestment, including, perhaps, all forms of both personal and real property. There are many practical advantages in permitting your executor-trustee to register securities in the name of a nominee or in a street name as it is sometimes called. This procedure simplifies both the purchase and sale of securities and might prevent a substantial loss in a fluctuating market.

If you own or expect your trust estate to own stocks, then your executor-trustee should be authorized to vote stocks, exercise options, and participate in reorganizations. If a bank is appointed as your original or as a successor executor and if you own stock in that bank, your executor-trustee should be authorized to both hold and acquire its own shares. But since in the election of the directors of a national bank, shares of its own stock held as trustee cannot be voted, you should include a direction as to how those shares shall be voted.

Interest rates and mortgages can be troublesome. If interest rates decline, your executor-trustee may have a problem with continuing to hold a high-interest note secured by a mortgage which constitutes a good investment. The borrower may want to pay off and get a loan at a lower rate elsewhere. Your executor-trustee should be authorized to reduce interest rates and to release mortgages.

Often there is a troublesome question as to whether a particular disbursement constitutes a current expense or an improvement to an asset. Your executor-trustee can be empowered to charge expenses to income or to principal.

Stocks are purchased not only because of dividends which may be declared but also because of the possibility of appreciation. Your executor-trustee may be authorized to credit appreciation to either an income or a principal account, and for the same purpose, he may be authorized to deduct proportionately over the term of the investment premiums paid for fixed-income investments.

Every executor-trustee should be authorized to borrow money. A loan may be needed to repair or replace an improvement or to pay debts, taxes, funeral expenses, and costs of administration. A power to borrow may avoid the forced liquidation of an asset in a declining market.

Every executor-trustee should be given the power to sell assets in your estate. What is a good investment now may not be a good investment when you die and certainly not throughout the term of any trust that you may create.

If you own land, your executor-trustee should be authorized to improve it, to subdivide it, and to lease it for a term extending beyond the duration of the trust, and if there is any possibility of there being oil or any other mineral under the land, special provisions should be included for the execution of leases and unitization of properties.

Preferably, your executor should be authorized to file a joint income tax return with your surviving spouse and be given broad powers to exercise rights under the Internal Revenue Code. For example, if you own stock in a closely held corporation which has made or may make a Subchapter S election (to be taxed as a partnership), your executor should be authorized to continue the election during administration of the estate and advised that when the trust created by you comes into existence, the election will be automatically cancelled unless (1) the trust is a qualified Subchapter S trust and the beneficiary makes the Subchapter S election within 60 days or (2) the stock is transferred to the beneficiary who files a consent to continue the Subchapter S election. He should also be given the power, when election is available, to deduct expenses on your death tax return or on fiduciary income or death tax returns.

These are not all the powers which should be or could be granted to an executor-trustee. In preparing a will or a trust agreement, a careful draftsman will review the complete range of possibilities, referring perhaps to any one of the large number of loose-leaf services and form books which have excellent checklists covering most, if not all, of the possibilities.

chapter 8

AVOID SURVIVORSHIP TITLES

For all practical purposes, there are four ways in which you might take title to your home: (1) in your name, (2) in your wife's name, (3) jointly as husband and wife with right of survivorship, and (4) in both of your names as tenants in common. If you hold title as joint tenants with right of survivorship, then upon the death of one of you, the survivor will own the entire property. On the other hand, if you hold title as tenants in common, then upon the death of one of you, the survivor will own an undivided one-half interest in the property and the other one-half interest will be disposed of either by will or by inheritance as a part of the estate of the deceased.

There is seldom a sensible excuse for a joint title with a right of survivorship, but there are countless reasons for avoiding these treacherous tax traps. Under the Economic Recovery Tax Act of 1981, whenever a husband and wife hold property by the entirety or as joint tenants with right of survivorship, the new law assumes that for estate tax purposes each owns one half of the property. When the first one dies, only one half of the property is taxed, but this may not be a bargain. Before the change in the law, because of the marital deduction, in most cases only one half would have been taxed anyhow. Second, if title is held in the name of either the husband or wife only, the marital deduction can be used to avoid tax on one half of the property, but the property will get a stepped-up basis for income tax purposes equal to its value on the date of death of the owner. For example, if a married couple owns a $100,000 home that cost them $25,000, under the new rules, one half of its value is included in the estate of the first to die, but the survivor gets a home for which the income tax basis will be $62,500 (one half of the original $25,000 cost plus $50,000 making a total of only $62,500 instead of a $100,000 basis).

This new rule does not apply to joint tenancies held by persons other than husband and wife. Then the entirety of the property is taxed in the estate of the first joint tenant to die with the exception (1) of that portion which a survivor can prove was paid for by the survivor and (2) when, upon creation of the joint tenancy, the transfer when made was subjected to a gift tax.

Somewhat the same hazards prevail under the death tax laws of most states. In some instances, the rule follows the federal practice. In others, the entirety of the value is taxed in the estate of the first to die, and in still others, one half of the value is taxed in the estate of the first to die. Again, there is a risk of paying a death tax twice upon the same property. In only a few states does a survivorship title avoid taxes in the estate of the first to die.

If a tenancy by the entirety or a joint tenancy with right of survivorship has been created between husband and wife, the arrangement, under the new tax law, can be changed without penalty. There is no gift tax imposed upon transfer from a husband to a wife, and as a consequence, title to the property may now be placed in the name of either.

The creation and the termination of joint tenancies between parties other than spouses have serious gift tax, estate tax, and income tax consequences some of which are not apparent even to the well-trained attorney.

Second, as we have already seen, the creation of joint tenancies often increases either income or death taxes, both state and federal.

Third, there is an income tax consequence. If income-producing properties, such as securities or realty rentals, are placed in a joint tenancy, one half of the income therefrom is taxed to each joint tenant. In states where, at lower rates, separate income tax returns may be filed, taxes are reduced by the husband and the wife each having separate sources of income, but this result can better be achieved by placing title exclusively rather than jointly in the name of a spouse.

No one should ever create or sever a joint tenancy without the advice of competent tax counsel. You may get into trouble if you try to do it alone.

There are other compelling reasons to avoid joint tenancies. First, if you are married and have minor children, you and your spouse could be killed in a common disaster. Expensive and restrictive guardianships would be necessary for your children, unless the survivor happened to have a will creating a trust for their protection.

Second, if you are married and do not have children, a question could arise as to whether you or your spouse died first in a common disaster. Jointly held property could go either to your family or to your spouse's family.

Some people, who have not considered these consequences, have carelessly called joint tenancies the "poor man's will." A better title would be the "poor man's trap."

To say this does not mean that all joint tenancies are burdened with inevitably tragic consequences. A small checking account for household purposes entails inconsequential risks and detriments. Second, if an estate consists only of a home, its contents, a car, and a small bank account and if there are children born of the marriage who have reached adult age, then joint tenancies with right of survivorship will avoid probate and seldom cause significantly larger death tax assessments. Then, too, if a living trust has been created, it might be wise for title in the few assets kept outside to be held jointly by husband, wife, and trustee to avoid probate. For example, title to a car could be held in the name of husband, wife, and trustee.

But joint tenancies with a right of survivorship are seldom practical and useful. Avoid them if you can, and if you have already made the mistake of creating them, seek professional advice now to get them unraveled before it is too late.

chapter 9

ORGANIZE YOUR BUSINESS

If you own an interest in a retail business, a service enterprise, a farm, or a small manufacturing operation, that investment may represent the largest asset of your estate. As a foundation for your estate plan, you may need to reorganize your business to save taxes, to limit liabilities, and to assure its survival in the event of your disability or death.

Almost every business is operated as a sole proprietorship, a partnership, or a corporation. In a sole proprietorship, you alone are the owner and manager, but in a partnership, someone else is contributing either capital or services. Either a sole proprietorship or a partnership can be incorporated. A sole proprietorship may be interrupted by illness and ended by death, and a partnership may be terminated by death or by the withdrawal of any one of the partners. The life of a corporation need never end. This fact does not mean that every business should be incorporated, but every businessman should at least consider the advantages and disadvantages of obtaining a corporate charter.

In a sole proprietorship, you are personally responsible for all of the debts of your business, and your business is also responsible for all of your debts created outside of the business. If on company business you or one of your employees should have the great misfortune to be at fault colliding with a school bus, injury and death claims in excess of your insurance coverages could total far more than your net worth.

In one case, a subcontractor entered into an agreement to erect guard rails on an interstate highway. The bid on the job was based upon quotations from suppliers, and after the bid was accepted, the subcontractor issued purchase orders which were accepted by the source of supply. Unfortunately, by the time work orders were issued, the supplier could not purchase raw materials at a price equal to the contract which he had made for the delivery of fabricated materials. The supplier notified the subcontractor that no further deliveries would be made except upon the basis of a 50 percent price increase. If the subcontractor paid the higher price, the loss on the project would exceed the subcontractor's net worth. If the subcontractor bought the guard rails on the open market, the price would be even higher than the new quotation from his old supplier. If the subcontractor failed to perform the contract, the prime contractor would complete performance and sue the subcontractor for the difference between the cost of performance and the contract price. Bankruptcy was inevitable, but fortunately the subcontractor was incorporated. His loss was limited to the assets he had invested in his business.

Some of the risks of carrying on a business cannot be insured at a premium which the business can afford to pay. Incorporation is the only practical means of limiting liability. Often, too, the corporate form can be structured to reduce income taxes significantly.

If you are operating a partnership without a written partnership agreement, do you know what might happen at your death? Death dissolves a partnership, and in most states unless a court intervenes, your surviving partner or partners will have the absolute right to liquidate the partnership. If you are carrying on your business as a corporation, the stock of which is closely held, your risks are almost equally great. If you own less than a majority of the stock, the surviving stockholders can decline to elect another member of your family to replace you as an officer and can adopt a small dividend policy so that your estate will realize less than it should from your investment.

If you are in a partnership, you need a partnership agreement. If you own stock in a closely held corporation, then you need an agreement among stockholders. In Chapter 10, we will see what plans you can make for continuing your business or for disposing of it at your death, but these moves are more than valuable tools in estate planning. Many of the problems of managing a business can best be dealt with by a contract among persons associated in the business. For example, in most states unless the powers of a partner are restricted by contract, any general partner may employ or fire any employee, borrow money on behalf of the partnership, carry on the usual business of the partnership, sign contracts, and convey real estate.

Many of these same risks exist in the operation of a closely held corporation. In such, however, powers of an officer can be limited by bylaws, and too, further limitations can be imposed by an agreement among stockholders. Of course, in drafting a stockholder's agreement, different language is used. In a partnership contract, partners agree to take certain steps and to refrain from other courses of action. In a stockholder's agreement, the stockholder is required to vote his stock in a particular way in the management of corporate affairs, but in both cases—the partnership contract and the stockholder's agreement—the same results can be achieved by similar techniques.

Why do so many partnerships fail? One of the major reasons is that many partnerships are organized upon the premise that profits and losses should be shared strictly on the basis of capital investment, but in every partnership, the abilities and the performances of partners differ. There is always the risk, too, that one member of a partnership will lose interest, become an alcoholic, suffer a disabling illness, or otherwise fail to carry his part of the load. In such event, disagreement, dispute, and dissatisfaction often begin—and may threaten to disrupt whatever plans you have made for your estate. The difficulty stems basically from a pattern of distributing profits entirely on the basis of capital investment. Such a division is fair and reasonable only in those rare instances in which the services of partners are rendered in the same proportion in which their capital has been contributed.

An equitable basis for dividing profits among partners is, therefore, one of the most important matters to be covered in a partnership agreement in order to protect your and your heirs' interests. There are many ways to meet the problem. Perhaps the most satisfactory is that of allocating a percentage of the profits to capital investments and a percentage of the profits to services. For example, it may be agreed that 50 percent of the net income of the partnership will be divided among those owning interests in the partnership in the percentage of their respective investments. The remaining 50 percent of the net income can then be divided among the partners contributing services to the partnership in proportion to the value of the work actually done by them. This basic percentage division should be predicated primarily upon the extent to which capital as distinguished from services will be responsible for the success of the enterprise. When the partnership agreement is first negotiated, it is far better to agree upon the initial division among the persons who are to contribute services, but there should always be some provision for changing this allocation over the years as circumstances require.

A second method of dividing profits between capital and management is to provide in the partnership agreement that salaries shall be paid to managing partners according to the job title held by each, that each partner will be elected to his job by all of the partners, and that the salaries will be reviewed and modified from time to time as necessary. The balance of the earnings after payment of salaries to management partners can be divided among those investing in the business in proportion to their capital contribution.

Either of these two arrangements for dividing profits can prove helpful in settling the questions which arise when a partner dies or becomes totally disabled. For example, a partner contributing services and having a capital investment would, upon death or disability, lose the right to draw that percentage resulting from services, but he or his estate might be permitted to retain an interest in the partnership, receiving therefrom only that part of the profits attributable to his capital invested. Chapter 10 will deal entirely with the sale of or the survival of the business upon your death.

Every partnership agreement should also contain some provision for dissolution of the partnership during the lifetime of the partners. Partners, like husbands and wives, do fall out with each other. A divorce can be obtained in a bitter and expensive lawsuit, and by the same token, a partnership can be dissolved by litigation. But only a fool would prefer a lawsuit to a well-planned method of settling differences. The largest asset of your estate could be placed in jeopardy or virtually destroyed.

Over the years, any one of three situations may develop in a partnership. First, one of the partners for his own good reasons may simply want out of the partnership. Second, for some very excellent reason or reasons, one or more of the partners may want to force another partner out. Third, there is the possibility of one or more of the partners wanting to force another out without having any good, sound business reason for the expulsion.

Many partnership agreements provide that if any partner wants to withdraw voluntarily from the partnership, then the remaining partner shall have an option to buy the interest of the retiring partner at the price set up for partnership valuation in the event of the death of a partner. If you prefer to discourage voluntary retirement of partners, then it can be provided instead that the buyout shall be at some discount, such as 10 percent off of the agreed valuation basis.

It is desirable but difficult to cover the situation arising when some partners want to force one of the other partners out either with or without a good and sufficient reason. If the partnership agreement provides for the expulsion of a partner for a specific cause, then some of the causes which may be listed are these: inactivity, disability, neglect of business, breach of partnership articles, or conflicting outside interests. If causes for expulsion are listed in a partnership agreement, it is advisable to have the partnership agreement contain an arbitration clause so that an outsider may make a finding as to whether or not an adequate cause for expulsion exists. Furthermore, if you adopt a provision for expulsion with cause, it is probably wiser to provide that a partner can be forced out even then only if a premium, which may be 10 percent or more above agreed valuation, is paid to the partner being forced out.

In lieu of the arrangements described, some partnership agreements simply provide that if any partner wants out or if any partner wants to force another out, then the entire partnership shall be transferred to those partners offering the highest price for the whole. This method, of course, often produced unfair results because a partner may not be in a financial position to protect himself in the event a dissolution occurs. Please understand that the suggested alternatives are not the only possibilities but that they are the ones most frequently encountered.

A well-written partnership agreement should also cover the situation which presents itself when one of the partners becomes either totally or partially disabled and thus is prevented from performing his management duties for the partnership. Sometimes it is provided that the disabled partner shall employ at his own expense a person suitable to the other partners to perform his duties during the period of his absence. Again, we sometimes find a provision that those partners who are able to work in the business shall then receive all of that percentage of the earnings distributable to management but that these partners must pay out of this percentage the salary of the highest paid employee of the partnership. Finally, of course, if a partner becomes disabled, the partnership can be dissolved, or there can be a renegotiation of the net income percentages to be received by the various members of the partnership.

The courts have adopted most peculiar rules with reference to partnerships. One of them is that in the absence of an agreement, unequal services by partners will be presumed to have been rendered without expectation of reward. This rule emphasizes the importance of having in a partnership agreement some provision for conduct of the partnership in the event of disability of a partner. Courts do not want to take on the task of looking into the question of whether one partner has performed the more onerous duties or been more skillful or industrious than the other. If you want to take care of your rights effectively, you can do it not by looking to the courts but only through means of a partnership agreement.

For example, in the absence of a partnership agreement, each partner has full control over partnership funds. A partner owning only a 10 percent interest in a business has full authority to make contracts, incur liabilities, and manage the business. Bearing in mind the unlimited liability of a partner for all partnership obligations, it is vitally important that every partnership agreement contain certain limitations upon the powers of a partner. Protection of your partnership investment is an essential part of estate planning and preservation.

Some of the prohibitions frequently included in a partnership agreement are: (1) purchasing or selling real estate or any other fixed asset without the consent of copartners, (2) signing a note or contracting any other debt for the partnership without the consent of copartners, (3) guaranteeing any commercial paper on behalf of the partnership without the consent of copartners, (4) signing a partnership check payable to himself, (5) borrowing money from the firm for personal use, (6) lending any money of the firm without the consent of copartners.

Many partnership agreements contain provisions concerning the hiring and firing of employees. For example, a partnership agreement might authorize only one of the partners to engage all employees to be paid by the hour and require consent of other partners to hire salaried personnel. Some partnership agreements also require consent of partners to discharge salaried personnel.

To avoid misunderstanding, some partnership agreements define the duties of the partners quite carefully. Whenever this is done, it is easier for an outsider to determine, in the event of a dispute, whether a particular partner is carrying his assigned portion of the work load.

A partnership agreement may well contain various other miscellaneous but important provisions. It is somewhat easier to justify
travel and entertainment deductions on income tax returns if they
are covered by the partnership agreement. Then, too, this is the
proper place to establish these allowances on a fair basis between or
among the partners.

Arguments sometimes arise concerning drawing accounts and the
distribution and retention of partnership profits. These matters, as
well as contributions to cover partnership losses, can best be dealt
with in the partnership agreement. A clause providing for an audit of
partnership books on the request of any partner is also a good idea
and an especially worthwhile one in the event of the death of a partner. An arbitration clause is usually a valuable addition to any partnership agreement.

If you have incorporated or later decide to incorporate your business, you will need bylaws, corporate resolutions, and an agreement
among stockholders taking care of many of the same problems that
arise in the conduct of a business as a partnership. The two main reasons to consider a corporation are the limiting of liabilities, thereby
conserving your estate, and the tax advantages to be gained, which
will increase the value of your estate.

A corporation has a decided advantage over other types of organizations in that its creditors are limited in the collection of their
claims to the assets of the corporation; they cannot reach the other
assets of its stockholders. Tax considerations, however, are often
paramount in determining whether a business should be incorporated or continued as a sole proprietorship or partnership.

The corporation is a separate taxpayer: It files its own income tax
return. Prior to 1982, the federal tax rate was 17 percent on the first
$25,000, 40 percent on the next $25,000, 30 percent on the next
$25,000, 40 percent on the next $25,000, and 46 percent on all over
$100,000. Beginning in 1982, the rates in the two lowest corporate
brackets will be (a) 16 percent of taxable income not in excess of
$25,000 and (b) 19 percent of taxable income in excess of $25,000
but not in excess of $50,000. In 1983 and later years, the rate of the
two lowest corporate brackets will be: (a) 15 percent of taxable income not in excess of $25,000 and (b) 18 percent of taxable income
in excess of $25,000 but not in excess of $50,000. On your own individual tax return, you will reflect as income any salary paid to you
by the corporation and any dividends which you receive from it.
The corporation can deduct, in computing its net income, all salaries
paid, but of course, it cannot deduct the dividends. Therefore, a tax

will have been paid by the corporation on its net income, and then you will be taxed again on any dividends paid to you by the corporation, with the exceptions to be discussed.

Prior to 1981, individual income tax rates ranged from a low of 14 percent to a high of 70 percent. In 1981, the tax reduction was only 1¼ percent of the tax otherwise imposed. In 1982, there is an across-the-board rate reduction of 10 percent, for 1983, an additional rate reduction of 10 percent, and for 1984, a further reduction of 5 percent. Beginning on January 1, 1982, the highest marginal tax rate dropped from 70 percent to 50 percent. Starting in 1985, individual rate brackets, the personal exemption, and the zero-bracket amount will be adjusted for inflation each year. If the corporation pays out in salaries to owners only as much money as they need to live on, retaining additional profits in the corporation, it is often possible that the combined earnings will be taxed at a lower rate.

First, if you incorporate a business, you can retain individual ownership of land, of improvements, and perhaps, even of fixtures and equipment. These can be leased to the corporation with the corporation being given an option to purchase. The rental, of course, will be deductible by the corporation and taxable to you, but later when profits have accumulated in the corporation, the option to purchase can be exercised and money taken out of the corporation in a form other than as a taxable dividend. One word of caution here, however: If, when the option is exercised, you, your spouse, your minor children, and your minor grandchildren own together over 80 percent of the corporate stock, any gain upon the sale of depreciable property will be ordinary income rather than a capital gain. With the accelerated cost recovery method of depreciation there is also an exposure to taxable depreciation recapture.

Another way to get tax-free money out of a corporation is to organize it with what is known as a thin capital structure. For example, if $60,000 will be required to finance operations initially, 25 percent of this sum could be procured by the issuance of common stock. The remaining $45,000 could be obtained in the form of a loan. As profits accumulate, these can be used to retire the loan.

A corporation without being subjected to a tax of 27½ percent or more upon unreasonable accumulation of surplus can build its retained earnings to a total of $250,000 beginning in 1982. Furthermore, surplus can exceed this level as long as the funds are employed in the business activities of the corporation. When expansion no longer makes sense and after the corporation has accumulated sufficient funds for retirement of debts, exercise of options, and the financing of its operations, the corporation may make a Subchapter S election (to be taxed as if it were a partnership instead of as a corporation).

Whenever you incorporate, you can transfer the assets of your sole proprietorship or of the partnership to the corporation in exchange for common stock, retaining in your business only enough in the way of assets to satisfy outstanding debts. This exchange of property for stock will be tax free.

When you incorporate, you may wish to enter into a stockholders agreement under Section 1244 of the Internal Revenue Code. To do so is simply protective. If the corporation should unfortunately be unsuccessful, then the entire loss in value of the common stock can be deducted against your ordinary income. If this election is not made, your deduction would constitute a long-term capital loss only half of which would constitute a deduction, and then each year, the amount of that loss which could be deducted would be $3,000.

Once again, this book is not a do-it-yourself manual. This book is only a checklist suggesting questions which you should explore. The object is not to determine whether or not you should incorporate your business or tell you how to do it. You are only being urged to review your business to determine with the advice of counsel what the best form for its organization would be and then to prepare either a partnership agreement or a stockholders agreement.

In estate planning, distribution of your estate at the lowest possible tax cost should not be the only objective. You must be equally concerned with building and conserving an estate to be enjoyed by you and your spouse in your retirement years.

chapter 10

PREPARE FOR THE SALE OR
SURVIVAL OF YOUR BUSINESS

If a substantial portion of your income is derived from a business and if that business represents a significant portion of your total estate, some provision for the continuation or the liquidation of that business is a most essential part of your estate planning. Your death will create problems of (1) authority to continue the business, (2) valuation of the business, and (3) personnel to manage the business. If you are the key man in the business, you are in a better position than anyone else to make a determination now for the solution of these critical problems.

If the business or your interest in the business is to be sold and if you are approaching retirement age, one solution is to sell the business during your lifetime. You may be in a better position than anyone else to negotiate satisfactory terms and price, but of course, you will have to consider the income tax consequence. If your cost basis is low compared with the prospective sale price, the adverse income tax consequence may preclude a lifetime sale.

Some businesses are readily marketable after the death of the owner. For example, the success of a liquor store is attributable more to its licenses and location than to management. Apartments, commercial buildings, and warehouses can be readily sold at market values established by comparable sales. Established formulas exist for the valuation of insurance agencies, radio and TV stations, and newspapers, but for most retail establishments, the determination of market value is a difficult task, and the identification of a buyer who will pay that price at what is virtually a distress sale is almost an impossibility. If you cannot either sell your business during your lifetime or negotiate a satisfactory buy-and-sell agreement effective at your death, however, then as a bare minimum, you should by your will empower your executor-trustee to sell and/or to operate the business and by letter or otherwise give him your best advice on how to value and how to dispose of the business.

Another alternative is to give your interest in the business to members of your family during your lifetime, especially if you have a child who is interested in and capable of taking over the enterprise. This end can ordinarily best be accomplished by either incorporating the business or reorganizing an existing corporation. For example, in the organizing or recapitalizing of a corporation, preferred stock can be issued representing substantially all of the equity and having all the voting rights. The common stock can be given or sold to a child or children who will reap the benefits of future business success. Another possibility is to give, sell, or will to a child interested in the business the common stock with voting rights while leaving the preferred stock as a part of a trust for your wife or other children.

More often than not, a buy-and-sell agreement is the only practical solution for disposing of a business interest. The agreement is usually made among partners or among all of the stockholders of a closely held corporation, but a buy-and-sell agreement effective at death can be made between a sole proprietor and either a member of his family or a key employee. In addition to providing for disposition of the business interest, a properly prepared agreement can control the estate tax valuation of the business interest. For that purpose it must (1) be an arm's-length transaction, (2) restrict the sale of the interest during the life of the seller unless first offered to the other contracting parties, and (3) either (a) give the survivor or survivors the option to buy at a price fixed by the agreement or (b) require the sale of the interest by the estate of the deceased and the purchase thereof by the other contracting parties. Alternatively, with a corporation, the contract can require the corporation itself rather than its other stockholders to purchase the interest of the deceased.

The valuation of any business is a matter of opinion. No one has ever devised a formula that would be applicable to every situation.

In negotiating a buy-and-sell agreement, you should remember that, after all, you may be the survivor. Because you do not know whether you will be the buyer or the seller, it is in your own interest to establish a fair and equitable basis for arriving at a price. If you should be the first to die, you want an assured purchaser at the negotiated price; and if one of your business associates should die first, then you need an assurance that you will be protected from unwanted outsiders.

You and your attorney should begin by finding out, if you can, the basis upon which similar business enterprises have been sold in recent years. For example, if your business is an insurance agency, the formula might be fixed assets plus some multiple of average commissions earned. Radio stations are ordinarily priced at fixed assets plus a multiple of annual billings. Net worth is seldom a safisfactory price basis because, after all, it is what a business earns that counts. For that reason, in many businesses, the capitalization-of-earnings method is employed. The sale price can be reached by determining the average net profit of the business for a term of anywhere from three to five years preceding the date of the sale and then multiplying the average by a figure which will produce the result upon which the average profit is a fair return.

Some businessmen prefer a buy-and-sell agreement with a schedule attached on which, at the end of each year, the parties agree upon a new business valuation, but even if that approach is used, the contract should contain a provision that if the parties fail to fix that value annually, a formula for valuation shall be used.

Finally, some contracts provide for valuation of the business by one or more experts. In some sections of the country, it is possible to identify, usually in the corporate finance department of a brokerage concern or the trust department of a large commercial bank, a man well trained in the valuation of business enterprises. The price can also be fixed by a compulsory arbitration provision.

Parties to the buy-and-sell agreement must make some arrangement to provide for the funds that will be needed to pay the purchase price. One possibility is that of allowing the buyers to make the payments on an installment basis with the term being spread over a period of 5 or perhaps even 10 years, with the deferred purchase price to bear interest and with the obligation to be secured by the assets sold. Alternatively, a fund can be created in advance for the purpose of carrying out the contract. In the latter case, however, there is a risk that death may occur before an adequate fund has been accumulated to effect the purchase. If this risk is to be avoided, then a practical method of providing funds is to purchase insurance to fund the buy-and-sell agreement in whole or in part. Premiums on these policies are not income tax deductions, but the insurance proceeds are income tax free.

There are a number of methods of purchasing business life insurance. If there are only two partners, each would normally want to insure the other's life in an amount sufficient to provide the purchase price set up in the buy-and-sell agreement. If there are several partners or stockholders, it is sometimes better to have the partnership or the corporation itself own the policies and pay the premiums. A third method is to use an insurance trust, which has advantages in a few situations.

One of the difficulties of a corporation accumulating earnings to fund a buy-and-sell agreement is the risk that accumulated earnings and profits will go beyond the reasonable needs of the business and become taxable at the rates imposed on accumulated taxable income.

The importance of the buy-and-sell agreement cannot be overemphasized. If you have been earning a salary as an officer of a closely held corporation, its board of directors may not elect another member of your family to replace you as an officer, and a small-dividend policy can be adopted so that your estate will realize very little from your investment. Upon your death, a partnership will be dissolved unless you have an agreement providing for its continuation.

chapter 11

REVIEW YOUR LIFE INSURANCE

Millions of dollars are wasted on life insurance, and some of that money may be yours. There are four reasons that the money may be wasted. First, ordinary life insurance (which combines pure insurance with savings) is all too often purchased when term insurance without a savings feature might offer better protection at a lower cost. Second, you may be a victim of the myth that all companies charge the same premium for like protection. Actually, the net cost of some policies is twice that of others. Third, you may purchase or carry life insurance which you do not need. Fourth, in an inflationary economy, you are suffering a constant loss of the purchasing power of the dollars invested in life insurance and savings.

Life insurance can be a valuable if not an essential part of your estate plan. Above all, you may need coverage to provide for the care of your family in the event of your premature death. Again, life insurance may be needed to pay debts, funeral expenses, costs of administration, and death taxes. Often, life insurance is the best way to fund a buy-and-sell agreement. Occasionally, life insurance serves better than anything else as a forced plan of savings. Life insurance has many other uses, too, but its primary purpose is to protect your dependents financially.

Never let anyone sell you life insurance. Buy it yourself to meet a specific need. If you do not have any dependents, you probably need little, if any, life insurance. If in the later years of your life you have accumulated an estate sufficient for the support of yourself and your wife and if you do not require insurance for some other valid purpose, such as payment of death taxes, you should seriously consider converting ordinary life insurance into paid-up insurance and perhaps dropping some of your term or pure insurance. If you are married, if your wife cannot support herself, if you have minor children, and if you have only a small estate, then your life insurance requirements are probably larger than they will be at any other time in your life. As you accumulate an estate of your own and your children complete their education, your life insurance requirements ordinarily will decline with each passing year. The constant change in your own financial and family circumstances suggests that your life insurance portfolio should be reviewed at least every five years.

In reviewing your life insurance program, you should begin by defining the needs of your dependents. How much insurance is needed to increase the size of your estate to a level that will support your family if you should die now? Of course, you may or may not be able to afford as much life insurance as you should have.

After you have projected the needs of your dependents, you should determine the availability of other funds to meet their requirements. To what extent can your wife or adult children support minor children? What social security benefits will be available? Here you do not have to guess. From your local social security office, you can obtain a Request for Statement of Earnings postcard to be mailed to the Social Security Administration, Baltimore, Maryland 21235. All you have to do is write on the postcard "Benefit estimate, please." Your local social security office also has free pamphlets explaining the benefits to which your family will become entitled, and your local social security representative will be glad to estimate the benefits that your wife and children would receive if you should die now. Your social security benefits are a very important part of your life insurance program, and you may be pleasantly surprised to find out the extent to which these will begin to meet the needs of your dependents.

Finally, you should take into consideration the other assets in your estate including those arising out of pension and profit-sharing plans. You may also have an expectancy of inheritance or it may be that some other member of your family could and would perform a part of your obligation to support those for whom you care.

Next, you need to consider the kind of life insurance that you should buy, and that decision necessitates your understanding exactly what life insurance is. The life history of a group of people can be predicted with a reasonable degree of accuracy. The combined experience of a group of life insurance companies reflects death rates per 1,000 shown in the accompanying table.

Age	Death rate per 1,000
25	1.25
35	1.40
45	3.96
55	11.00
65	27.99
75	63.36
85	149.17

If there were no costs of administering an insurance program, each of 1,000 people at age 35 would have to pay $1.40 per year to provide $1,000 for each person in the group who died. By age 55, the cost would jump to $11 per year per person.

For term or pure insurance, you need to pay a premium equal to the risk of death at a given age level plus the cost to the insurance company of administering the program and making a profit. In a sense, term insurance is like fire insurance. If you assume that there are 1,000 homes in a town, each worth $20,000, and that only one home will burn per year, each person would have to contribute only $20 to provide a common fund sufficient to pay for that single loss. When you buy either fire insurance or term life insurance, you pay a premium only for the actual risk of loss plus expenses and a profit to the company.

Ordinary life insurance and the many variations thereof, including endowment insurance, 20-pay life, and many, many others, consists of two elements: term life insurance plus a savings feature. For example, with an ordinary life policy, 12.5 cents of your premium dollar may pay for protection, 46.8 cents savings, 26 cents anticipated dividends, and 14.7 cents the company's expenses and profit. The relationship of these elements in a $25,000 straight life policy issued at age 35 is illustrated in the diagram shown below.

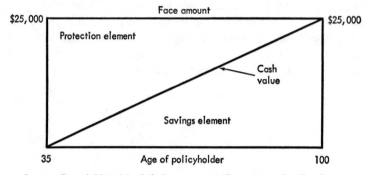

Source: Joseph M. Belth, *Life Insurance: A Consumer's Handbook* (Bloomington: Indiana University Press, 1973), p. 23.

The savings element of an ordinary life policy is called its cash value, and ordinarily that amount can be borrowed at any time from the insurance company with interest thereon. Because the cash value is constantly growing, the protection element is steadily declining. If you die, your beneficiary will receive the face amount of the policy, but a substantial part of the proceeds will represent monies that you have saved and on which the insurance company has paid a very small rate of interest, ranging, probably, from 2 to 5 percent. For this reason alone, ordinary life insurance is seldom a good investment. You can take the difference between the premium for term insurance and the premium for ordinary life insurance and invest in a savings account producing a much larger return than you will get from a life insurance company. Admittedly, there is no income tax on the interest paid by a life insurance company on the savings deposited with it, but unless you are in a very high income tax bracket, you will make more after taxes by doing your own savings than by letting an insurance company save your money for you.

Another delightful aspect of term insurance is that the premium costs are based upon your age, as is illustrated by the chart shown below comparing premiums for straight life and five-year renewable term policies issued in 1970 to men age 35 by Connecticut Mutual Life Insurance Company.

Your greatest insurance needs will probably be during the years when your children are growing up. By purchasing one-year or five-

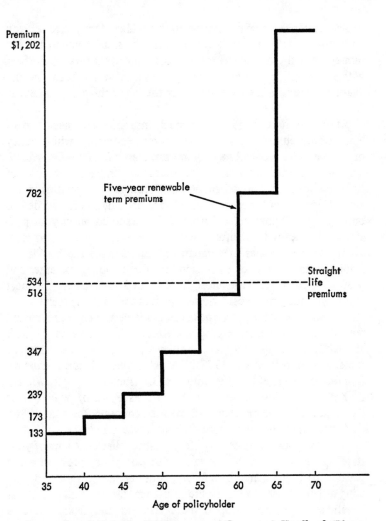

Source: Joseph M. Belth, *Life Insurance: A Consumer's Handbook* (Bloomington: Indiana University Press, 1973), p. 27.

year renewable term, you can afford a much larger portfolio of life insurance. By the time the cost of term insurance becomes much higher, you probably will be better able to afford the increased premiums, or perhaps you can reduce the amount of insurance carried. After all, if you purchase ordinary life insurance, that is exactly what is happening every year: As your savings increase through the ordinary life policy, the amount of pure insurance being purchased through that policy declines.

An insurance company representative will seldom try to sell you term insurance: The agent's commissions are small compared to the money he will make by selling you ordinary life insurance. In fact, with ordinary life insurance, the agent usually gets at least the first year's premium as his fee for making the sale if the policy is kept in force.

After you have decided how much insurance you need and of what kind, you need to select the insurance company whose policy or policies you would like to purchase. *Best's Review, Life/Health* edition, published monthly, rates insurance companies in terms of financial strength. Out of about 2,000 companies operating in the United States, its "most favorable" recommendation is awarded to only about 130 companies. Preferably, you should select your policies from one of these after having made a premium comparison. There are many bases of comparison, but perhaps the best is the amount retained out of each premium for company expenses and profits. Among even the most highly rated companies, the most expensive policy may cost twice as much as the least expensive.

Fortunately, some good books are available to help you plan and review your life insurance program. Among them are these: Joseph M. Belth, *Life Insurance: A Consumer's Handbook* (Bloomington: Indiana University Press, 1973); *The Consumers Union Report on Life Insurance* (1980) by the Editors of Consumers Reports; William B. Kirby, *Life Insurance from the Buyer's Point of View* (Great Barrington, Mass.: American Institute for Economic Research, 1980).

A few other comments about life insurance may be helpful. First, in purchasing and in reviewing life insurance, check the laws of your state. If there is a death tax exemption for policy proceeds made payable to a designated beneficiary, consider the possibility of creating a living trust funded by life insurance. Do not name minors as beneficiaries. A trusteeship is more efficient and flexible than a guardianship.

When you have accumulated an estate of your own sufficient to support your dependents and to pay all the costs of settling your estate, consider the possibility of converting ordinary life insurance into paid-up insurance, which means that you take a lower amount of coverage but no longer have to pay premiums. At that stage in life, some or all of your term or pure insurance may be dropped.

If you have a mortgage on your home, by all means consider buying credit life insurance or the equivalent which will pay off the loan in the event of your death. Preferably, if you live in a state where life insurance to a designated beneficiary is exempt from death taxes, you should purchase declining-value term insurance payable to a designated beneficiary rather than to a creditor.

You probably will not need certain kinds of insurance. If your wife works and helps support your children, then perhaps you do need life insurance for her; but if there is no earning power to be replaced by her death, the life insurance requirements are much smaller. You should consider only the cost of final expenses in her estate, including funeral expenses and perhaps the cost of hiring someone else to take care of your house and children. In most cases, however, insurance dollars can better be placed in the husband's program than in the wife's. Certainly the husband's should be accorded higher priority.

The premiums for accident insurance are small because the risk of death through casualty is relatively meager, but your insurance program should be based upon your needs for insurance, and those certainly do not increase simply because you die an accidental rather than a natural death. If you want accident insurance, it can probably be purchased cheaper as an addition to your ordinary life or term insurance policy.

If you have ordinary life insurance, do not overlook the possibility of borrowing the cash value. At times the interest which you will have to pay the life insurance company will be substantially less than the interest or dividends which you can earn by investing the money elsewhere. Life insurance cash values are also a useful source of a loan to meet emergencies. Interest rates are often less than those charged by lending institutions.

By all means, consider the possibility of putting a waiver-of-premium rider on your life insurance policies. By doing so, you provide that premiums no longer have to be paid after the policy holder has become disabled.

Review your life insurance program every five years. Measure what you hold against the current needs of your dependents. Consider the possibility of changing a beneficiary designation. Determine whether ordinary life insurance should be converted to paid-up insurance and term coverage dropped or reduced. Do not assume that your insurance needs are static and constant. Keep your insurance program up-to-date.

chapter 12

THINK BEFORE YOU GIVE

You can save money by giving it away. Although gifts in excess of exemptions are taxable, increases in the value of the property which occur after the gift will not be included in your estate. Also, by giving income-producing property, you will reduce your own income tax liability. But before making any substantial gift, you should do more than consider the tax consequences. For a variety of reasons, you should think twice before giving a substantial part of your estate away.

First, you should not make any gifts that will reduce your estate below the level needed for the support of yourself and your wife. Never forget that you will need income from investments after your retirement and that either you or your wife may suffer a long and expensive illness. Furthermore, tax savings from gifts may be inconsequential unless your estate is substantially in excess of the amount shown on page 60.

Giving to a child whose marriage may break up can prove costly. Your son's total estate will affect the alimony he has to pay, and your daughter's net worth will be a factor in the alimony she can collect.

Certainly, too, you would not want to make a large gift to a child who has not demonstrated sufficient maturity and acumen to man-

Year	Single person	Married person
1982	$225,000	$ 450,000
1983	275,000	550,000
1984	325,000	650,000
1985	400,000	800,000
1986	500,000	1,000,000
1987	600,000	1,200,000

age his or her own estate, nor should you risk a gift of an interest in a closely held business (a partnership or a corporation) to a child or a stepchild who might become alienated from you.

On the other hand, there are many compelling reasons why gifts should be made. First, if you can afford them, by all means make gifts to your children while you are living and can have the pleasure of seeing them enjoy your generosity. If you are not wealthy enough to make a major gift, you can often lend your credit to a child by becoming a cosigner on a promissory note, the proceeds of which are to be used to purchase a home or to establish a business. It is a lot of fun to see your children enjoy life while they have the time and the vitality to have the good times that you may have missed with your own struggle for survival.

Second, you can achieve almost unbelievable tax savings. You can give $10,000 a year to as many people as you like without being taxed, and if your wife lets one half of the gift be attributed to her, together you can give $20,000 a year per person without any tax. This is called an annual exclusion. Generally, but not invariably, unrestricted gifts of $10,000 or less per year per donee (other than gifts of life insurance) whenever made will not be brought back into your estate when you die. Only the amount over $10,000 per donee will be brought back into your estate. Therefore, if you want to make a gift to a child in the amount of $20,000, preferably you should make a gift of $10,000, and your spouse should make a gift of $10,000. In all probability, although a regulation has not been issued, this can be achieved by your first making a gift to your husband or wife. Under the Economic Recovery Tax Act of 1981, a gift from one spouse to another can be made in any amount without being subjected to the gift tax.

Those who can afford to be exceptionally generous should also consider the possibility of creating an irrevocable living trust for each grandchild, with the income from the trust to be distributed to or for the benefit of the grandchild until the grandchild reaches 21 years of age. The principal amount of each annual gift through the trustee for the benefit of the grandchild must be distributed only if the guardian for the grandchild demands distribution within the year in which the gift is made or upon the attainment of legal age by the grandchild whether that be 18 or 21. Most grandparents try to discourage withdrawals of principal by explaining that whenever a withdrawal is made, the grandparent shall not make any further gifts to the trustee for the benefit of the grandchild.

Finally, after the annual exclusion is exhausted, additional tax-free gifts may be made by utilizing the unified credit which may be taken either against a gift tax or the estate tax. This credit ranges from an exemption equivalent of $225,000 in 1982 to $600,000 in 1987.

Anyone who can afford to make enormous gifts may find it advantageous to make them. In the first place, earnings realized from the property that is given away will be taxed to the person receiving the property which, in most cases, will be taxed at a lower rate and which, in all cases, will take the accumulation of earnings out of the donor's estate.

For those who can afford to make major gifts, this is an opportunity to achieve the joy and gratification of providing funds for a grandchild's education. On the other hand, this simple fact of life should not be overlooked: children and grandchildren can be spoiled rotten by receiving too much too soon. For example, a father who could afford to give his son a sum sufficient to purchase office furniture, equipment, and a library needed to open a law practice very wisely lent his son the money that he needed and made him pay it back. He taught his son the value of a dollar which is worth far more in the development of character and enterprise than a generous gift which can destroy initiative.

A well-designed program of gifts reduces state death taxes as well as federal death taxes, gives the donor the pleasure of seeing his children and grandchildren have the good things of life while they are young enough to enjoy them, teaches them to manage investments, and yet, with appropriate safeguards, can limit the risk of making the child or grandchild a worthless spendthrift.

For example, when a child marries, you may wish to make a gift of a home. You and your wife, having each invested one half of the cost, could arrange for a $100,000 house to be conveyed to your daughter in exchange for 10 notes in the amount of $10,000 each, with five being payable to you and five being payable to your wife. Each year, you and your wife could forgive one of the notes held by each of you. At the end of five years, you would have given your child $100,000, and you would not have utilized any of your lifetime exemption equivalents. This plan, of course, will not work if the Internal Revenue Service can prove that you intended at the outset to cancel two notes each year.

In all probability, you will never want to make gifts in excess of the annual exclusions, one half of your adjusted gross estate to your wife and the exemption equivalents. When a gift exceeds these amounts, a tax upon the gifts will be imposed during your lifetime, and you will lose the use of that tax money. There are exceptions, of course. If you should make a gift to your children of any property which increases enormously in value during the remainder of your lifetime, then from a tax point of view, your children and you might be better off if a gift tax were paid during your lifetime. After all, the gift tax itself reduces the size of your estate.

Fortunately, there is another way that you can help your children without making any gifts. For example, you can make loans to them without charging them any interest on the loans. You could also buy a house for a child and permit the child to occupy the house rent free. You could transfer title to the house from yourself to your child by your will rather than by a deed, and the tax then would not be imposed until your death.

Whenever a gift is made, the tax is computed on the market value of the donated property, but in the hands of the donee if the property is sold for a profit, the gift retains your cost basis plus the gift tax. For example, if without having to pay any gift tax, you should give your children common stock which cost you $50,000 but which has a market value of $100,000, and if your children should sell the stock, they would have to pay a capital gain tax. For that reason, it is ordinarily preferable to make gifts of property having a cost basis to you approximately equal to market value. If you do not have any property of that kind, then the gift could well be a property which the donee would never want to sell in any event, or if the property must be sold, it is in some instances better to give the property to be sold as a gain to a donee who is in a lower income tax bracket than you are. Certainly, assets which are selling below their costs to you should not be used for gifts. It would be wiser to realize the capital loss and to make a gift of the proceeds.

If one of the principal reasons for the gift is to reduce your income taxes, then if there is a choice of assets, those producing the greater income might be the most desirable gifts. Although death taxes cannot always be reduced by a gift to your wife, if you live in a state imposing state income taxes, then occasionally, a gift of income-producing assets to your wife will reduce your total income tax bill. In such a case, however, the effect upon death taxes should also be considered, and your wife certainly should also make her own will. In fact, whenever you make a gift, the donee's will should be reviewed. It would be foolish to make a gift to children and risk having it come back to you upon the death of a child who has left no surviving spouse or children.

One gift which will not deprive you of any income and yet will save death taxes is a gift of life insurance made more than three years prior to the date of your death. It is easily valued, and the present value of the policy is much less than its maturity value. This gift also removes the face value from the top of your estate tax bracket.

If you are reluctant to make a gift because of the gift tax involved, you can select an asset which the donee can sell, and you can require the donee to pay the gift tax out of the proceeds of sale.

Another useful gift is that of an asset which can be expected to appreciate rapidly in value. For example, if you are starting a new business for which you expect phenomenal growth, you can give stock in that business before an earning pattern has been established. If that stock were retained throughout your lifetime, its value in your estate could be substantial, but by getting rid of that asset during your lifetime, you may succeed in taking valuable property out of your estate when you die.

Some gifts do not remove assets from your estate for death tax purposes. For example, if you reserve a life estate in the asset, the gift will not be effective until your death. Next, if you make a gift in excess of the annual exclusion, the excess will be included in your estate.

Never make a gift of over $10,000 to any one donee without the advice of counsel. First, a gift tax return must be filed. Second, you may need expert assistance in valuation of the gift. Third, the gift is an important part of your estate plan and also of the donee's estate plan. Both wills would be reviewed. Finally, if you make a gift to one child and not to another, you may want to include a provision in your will concerning advancements: In dividing up your estate among your children, you may in effect, want to add the gift back in before making the division and then deduct the gift from the share of the particular donee in the final settlement of your estate.

There is one other type of gift which will not save any death taxes but may have important income tax advantages. If you are supporting one of your parents, a mother-in-law, a father-in-law, or any other person, you can create what is known as a Clifford trust, placing property in it which will earn enough income to take care of the support which you are furnishing to someone else. To accomplish your tax purposes, the trust must last for 10 years or until the earlier death of the donee, but under a properly drafted agreement, you do not pay an income tax on the trust income. The trust beneficiary can deduct medical expense against the income and pay tax on the balance, if any, at a lower rate. A Clifford trust can also be used for other purposes, but this one application has proven to be the most valuable of all.

A person creating a Clifford trust should be aware of the fact that a gift tax return must be filed, but both the annual exclusion and the exemption equivalent may be used to offset the value of the income interest for the term of years being transferred to the gift beneficiary.

chapter 13

ASSEMBLE THE FACTS

Before having an estate-planning conference with your attorney, assemble all the facts concerning your estate and your family. Unless he has the most intimate details of your finances and of your family relationships, he cannot be expected to plan your estate properly. Furthermore, most attorneys charge for estate planning on the basis of the time devoted to the project. If you organize your information adequately, you will not only get a better estate plan but you will also substantially reduce its cost.

First, you should give him your complete name including nicknames and initials which are sometimes used, together with your home and your business addresses. He will need your date of birth and preferably your medical history.

For your wife, your children, their spouses, your grandchildren, and all other dependents for whom you intend to make some provision, you will also need the complete name, address, birth date, and condition of health of each. After all, greater accuracy in names and relationships can be achieved by writing all of these out in advance, and some special provision may have to be made in your estate plan for anyone who is disabled. The more you are willing to tell your attorney about the financial status, character traits, needs, and prospects of your beneficiaries, the better the job he can do for you.

Approximating your gross estate

Types of property	(1) Husband's	(2) Jointly held* Paid for by husband	(3) Jointly held* Paid for by wife	(4) Wife's
Liquid assets				
Cash on hand	$	$	$	$
Checking accounts				
Savings accounts				
Certificates of deposit				
Corporate stocks				
Mutual funds				
Corporate bonds				
U.S. Treasury bonds				
Municipal bonds				
Receivables				
Other quick assets				
Real estate				
Equity in homes	$	$	$	$
Income producing realty				
Unimproved realty				
Personal property				
Autos	$	$	$	$
Sporting equipment				
Furniture and household effects				
Jewelry and silverware				
Apparel and personal effects				
Art objects				
Collections				
Hobby equipment				

	Beneficiary Spouse	Estate	Other	
Personal insurance				
On testator's life	$ ( )	( )	( )	$
On lives of others	( )	( )	( )	
Annuities	( )	( )	( )	

Approximating your gross estate *(continued)*

	(1)	(2)	(3)	(4)
			Beneficiary	
			Es-	
		Spouse	*tate*	*Other*

Employee and retirement benefits

	(1)	(2)	(3)	(4)
Pension	$_____	( )	( )	( ) $_____
Profit sharing	_____	( )	( )	( ) _____
Other deferred compensation	_____	( )	( )	( ) _____
Stock options	_____	( )	( )	( ) _____
Savings and thrift plans	_____	( )	( )	( ) _____
Keogh retirement plans	_____	( )	( )	( ) _____
Individual retirement accounts	_____	( )	( )	( ) _____
Other	_____	( )	( )	( ) _____

	(1)	(2)	(3)	(4)
			Jointly held*	
		Paid	*Paid*	
	Hus-	*for by*	*for by*	
Types of property	*band's*	*husband*	*wife*	*Wife's*

Business interests

Sole proprietorships	$_____	$_____	$_____	$_____
Partnerships	_____	_____	_____	_____
Closely held corporations	_____	_____	_____	_____

Miscellaneous

Expectancies	$_____	$_____	$_____	$_____
Powers of appointment	_____	_____	_____	_____
Interests in trust funds	_____	_____	_____	_____
Royalties and patents	_____	_____	_____	_____
Oil, gas and mineral interests	_____	_____	_____	_____
Other	_____	_____	_____	_____
Current value of total assets	$_____	$_____	$_____	$_____

Husband's approximate gross estate (col. 1 + col. 2)	$_____ _____	
Wife's approximate gross estate (col. 3 + col. 4)		$_____ _____

Approximating your gross estate *(concluded)*

	Husband's	Wife's
Gross estate valuation	$_____	$_____
Deduct:		
1. Personal and joint liabilities and debts (notes, insurance loans, mortgages, taxes owing, etc.)	$_____	$_____
2. Funeral and last illness expenses	_____	_____
3. Probate and administration expenses	_____	_____
Total:	$_____	$_____
Approximate adjusted gross estate (gross estate less above deductions)	$_____	$_____

*Jointly held property interests should be listed one half to husband and one half to wife without reference to how the title is held, but for estate planning purposes, it is helpful to know who paid for the property.

If there are any property agreements between you and either your present wife or a former wife, he will need to see these.

You may not know whether title to real estate is held by you individually, as a joint tenant, or as a tenant in common. If you have any doubt about it, it is far wiser to take every one of your deeds to your estate-planning conference. You should also examine your securities to determine how title to each one is held, and here again if you have any doubt, take every one of them to the conference. Your attorney will also definitely need to know the cost and present market value of each.

Your estate planner will also need to have all of your life insurance policies, partnership agreements, stockholder agreements, pension plans, profit-sharing plans, stock options, and deferred compensation agreements. Preferably, before the conference, you should determine the status of your social security account.

If you hold any powers of appointment, your attorney must have a copy of each power and information concerning the appointive property. If you are already the beneficiary under a probated will or a trust, or if you have any expectancies of inheritance, this information, too, is vital.

If you have made any gifts in the past, these should be disclosed, and if gift tax returns have been filed, copies should be made available to your estate planner. Certainly you should take him copies of income tax returns for the three preceding years.

Finally, before going to an estate-planning conference, you should prepare a current balance sheet for yourself and for your wife. The form on pages 66-68 indicates some of the details required.

If you own a residence in more than one state, your attorney may wish to advise with you concerning acts which you may take to establish legal residence in the state that has the most favorable income and death tax structure. For example, Florida imposes as a death tax only the minimum amount allowable on the U.S. estate tax return as a credit for state death taxes, and Florida does not have any income taxes.

If you can, decide before your estate-planning conference what disposition you want made of automobiles, boats, trailers, household effects, hobby equipment, collections, objects of art, and apparel and personal effects. In all probability, you will want to give these to members of your family and not make them a part of any trust under your will.

If you are supporting your parents, your wife's parents or anyone else, then your attorney needs to know your plans for them upon your death. You should also be prepared to share with him your hopes and expectations for your wife, children, and others for whom you care so that he may work with you in developing a plan to meet their needs. If you also plan a charitable bequest, you should take with you the full name of the institution or institutions which you want to share in your estate.

chapter 14

SELECT AN ATTORNEY

Any attorney can write a will, but comparatively few are qualified to design an estate plan. Finding an expert is difficult. Lawyers cannot advertise their specialties although action to allow such advertising is presently being considered by the American Bar Association. The legal rating services rate attorneys on their overall abilities but not on their competence in a particular field.

There are tens of thousands of income tax, estate tax, and gift tax rulings every year. Every attorney cannot be expected to keep up with all of these, and yet unless he at least reads the advance sheets weekly which summarize each of these, he cannot hope to develop or to retain a competence in estate planning. Furthermore, the best books on estate planning are long, forbidding treatises covering sophisticated techniques which are understood only by a very select few. For most lawyers, estate planning is only a small part of the total practice of law, and any particular lawyer can hardly be expected to possess an expertise in every phase of his professional practice.

Unfortunately, too, there is a common conviction that the cost of estate planning is excessive. That inaccurate view has discouraged many a person from seeking professional advice. Actually, a competent attorney can almost invariably save a client in taxes many, many times the cost of developing a program for his estate. If the demand for estate-planning services ever reaches its potential, many more attorneys will become versed in the art of developing plans for distribution of property to the object or objects of one's affection at the least possible tax cost.

Meanwhile, the identification of an estate-planning expert is in and of itself an awesome task, but there are avenues of inquiry which should aid you in finding someone near you. *The Bar Register*, published annually, includes only those "lawyers who enjoy fine professional reputations." No other publication confines its listings "to the outstanding members of the Bar." Not every listee in *The Bar Register* is a preeminent estate-planning specialist, nor are all those not listed without competence in this specialized field. Nevertheless, if you begin with *The Bar Register*, you have increased immeasurably in your favor the odds of your finding one of the best.

The Martindale-Hubbell Law Directory lists every lawyer in the United States and rates his legal ability with the explanation: "The Legal Ability Ratings are 'a' (very high), 'b' (from high to very high) and 'c' (from fair to high). Minimum periods following admission to practice are not required for these ratings."

In the biographical section of the same publication, subscribers may publish cards reflecting, among other things, legal education, public offices held, association memberships, and publications. An attorney whose credits reflect that he has published or lectured in the field of estate planning may be your best choice. Both *The Bar Register* and *The Martindale-Hubbell Law Directory* are available in law school libraries and in the offices of most of the "a" and "b" rated lawyers.

If you are fortunate enough to live near a law school, a member of the faculty may be able to help you identify an estate-planning expert. Trust officers of banks are certainly in an excellent position to know those who are best qualified, but in smaller towns particularly, there are few expert trust officers and many of these are tempted to recommend whoever happens to be general counsel for the bank. Some probate judges and some probate clerks are experienced enough to differentiate between lawyers who write wills and attorneys who specialize in estate practice.

Regrettably, you may be compelled to make your choice by relying upon your own ability to differentiate between the tyros and the experts. You should not hesitate to ask your prospective counsel to show you his library. If he does not have a complete loose-leaf service (11 volumes, more or less) on income taxes, gifts taxes, and estate taxes, he will probably be a very poor choice. Preferably his library or another to which he has access should also contain all of the federal tax decisions.

Almost every estate-planning expert subscribes to, reads, and retains in his office copies of the Research Institute of America, Inc.'s *Estate Planning Alert* and Warren, Gorham & Lamont's magazine *Estate Planning*. He should also have one or more treatises on estate planning and, especially, all or one of the following loose-leaf services: The Research Institute of America, *Estate Planning and Taxation Coordinator*, Commerce Clearing House, *Financial and Estate Planning*, Prentice-Hall, *Successful Estate Planning*. You should not hesitate to ask to borrow recent issues of any of these and one of the estate-planning books on the pretense of needing them to formulate your ideas before the first estate-planning conference. If none of these publications is available, you had better try to find an attorney someplace else.

In a small town, you can go to a probate clerk's office and examine wills recently admitted to probate. The attorneys who are still writing one- and two-page wills should be stricken from your list of prospects. You may be surprised to discover how easy it is for you to determine which members of the bar are the more sophisticated draftsmen.

Doctors, at least, have been wise enough to identify specialties within their profession, and those who have passed their board qualifying examinations are probably adequate practitioners of their respective specialized arts. Unfortunately for the public, an infallible technique has not been developed for singling out the attorneys who are specialists in any particular field, excepting only patent and trademark specialists.

chapter 15

GET A LEGAL CHECKUP

Have you had a legal checkup lately? Most of us have a dental examination annually, an eye examination every few years, and a complete physical examination at least occasionally. Health is more important than property, but wisdom dictates the preservation of both. Estate planning, as, hopefully, you have discovered, is far more than employing someone to write a will. It is the art of designing a program for the effective management, enjoyment, and disposition of your property at the least possible tax cost, not only at your death but also during your lifetime.

As a part of your estate planning, you may want to ask your attorney to give you a complete legal audit. That would include not only your life insurance but also your fire insurance, casualty insurance, and health insurance programs. Have you ever made a list of your risk-of-loss exposures and compared these with your insurance coverages? The odds are that you will discover some enormous gaps. For example, on your automobile policy, are you carrying adequate liability coverage? All too many policies are written with limits of only $10,000 per person and $20,000 per accident, but judgments of $100,000 or more are becoming exceedingly common. For an amazingly small additional premium, you can increase your liability limits for bodily injury to $100,000 per person and $300,000 per occurrence. It is better to spend insurance dollars to achieve protection against major losses than in any other way.

Furthermore, your automobile property damage liability coverage should also be increased. If you were to be involved in a collision with a bus, a truck, or any vehicle with a valuable cargo, the usual $5,000 or $10,000 coverage would be grossly inadequate. Once again for a small additional premium, you can increase your property damage liability coverage to $50,000 or $100,000 per accident.

In an automobile policy, collision coverage (which takes care of damage to your own car) is relatively expensive, but if you can afford to pay the small losses yourself, you can reduce the premium materially by increasing the deductible amount (the portion of the loss to be borne by you) to at least $500. For a small cost, automobile coverages can include medical payments to each person injured, additional family protection coverages, and protection against losses caused by an uninsured motorist.

If you are engaged in the practice of any profession, you should carry a professional liability policy, and here again it is often possible to reduce the premium cost by providing for a deductible amount, being the loss to be borne by you. If you are engaged in business, you should have a comprehensive liability policy, a workman's compensation policy, and, possibly, business interruption coverage. These policies should be reviewed, too, upon a legal audit.

Today, the risk of loss by fire of a home, apartment, or business building is best covered under a multiperil policy which takes care not only of loss by fire but of many losses to persons and property occasioned by other casualties. With inflation increasing the cost of replacement of any structure, the amount of fire coverage should be reviewed annually.

On a homeowner's or other multiperil policy, liability limits can be increased to $100,000 per person and $300,000 per occurrence for a very nominal additional premium. If you use your home also for some office activities, an endorsement covering that use should be included on your homeowner's policy. A mysterious disappearance endorsement and a credit card endorsement are also good buys.

If you do not have one, you should certainly consider purchasing an "umbrella" policy to supplement all of your individual policies. After your underlying liability coverages have been exhausted by a claim, an umbrella policy protects up to a limit of perhaps $1 million or more. For example, if you are carrying an automobile liability of $100,000 per person and $300,000 per occurrence for bodily injury liability and if claims against you exceeded those amounts, then your umbrella policy would take care of the catastrophic excess. The umbrella policy would supplement your liability not only on your automobile policy but also on your professional liability, on your comprehensive liability, on your homeowner's policy, and on all other underlying coverages. Small commercial risks are now written with $500 as the minimum three-year premium and personal coverage for executives and professionals may be only $270 for three years with a $1 million limit and $540 for three years with a $5 million limit.

In health coverage, the average layman has neither the training nor the experience to compare available coverages and measure the reasonableness of premium cost. Exceptions, exclusions, waiting periods, and durations of coverage limit the benefits of many of the policies being sold. If you are unwilling to seek professional guidance on what policy to buy, you had better stick to Blue Cross-Blue Shield for basic protection and then supplement that with Blue Cross-Blue Shield or other major medical which takes care of 75 percent or more of the cost of a major illness over and above a deductible amount, which usually is covered by the basic Blue Cross-Blue Shield. After you become eligible for medicare, you should also purchase from the Social Security Administration Supplementary Medical Insurance and Blue Cross-Blue Shield comprehensive coverage supplementing medicare.

A legal checkup often includes a review of leases. Whether you are renting a house, an apartment, or a storeroom, the odds are that your lease can be improved by a supplemental lease, amended lease, or renewal lease.

If you carry automobile collision insurance, you may know that in the event of an accident, your insurance company will settle your loss with you and then take assignment of your right to sue the operator of the other vehicle involved in the accident. In effect, your insurance company takes over your right to recover from the person who hit you. This arrangement applies to other types of insurance. For example, some years ago, a tenant conducting a grocery business negligently caused the premises to be destroyed by fire. The landlord's insurer promptly paid the landlord, accepted an assignment of right to recover, sued the tenant for the loss, and recovered.

Almost every fire results from negligence, and either the landlord or the tenant in a particular building may be responsible for the blaze. Of course, legal liability insurance can be purchased to cover this risk, but unfortunately the premiums are substantial. This risk or loss can be eliminated by the simple process of obtaining a waiver of indemnity rights. In many states, a mutual waiver may be included in a lease without there being any increase in the cost of the insurance carried by either the landlord or the tenant. If, however, a lease does not contain a waiver of indemnification right, then both the landlord and the tenant need to protect themselves by carrying legal liability insurance.

Every existing lease and every new lease that is written should contain the following provisions:

> The Lessor waives and releases its right of indemnity against the Lessee for damages to its property (by fire or other casualty) occasioned by the negligence of the Lessee, its agents or employees, to the extent that the Lessor receives actual payment therefor under the Lessor's insurance policies. The Lessee waives and releases the Lessee's right of indemnity against the Lessor for damages to the Lessee's property (by fire or other casualty) occasioned by the negligence of the Lessor, its agents or employees, to the extent that Lessee receives actual payment therefor under Lessee's insurance policies.

Many insurance policies permit this agreement without notice to the insurance company, but preferably both the landlord and the tenant should advise their own insurance carriers that leases do contain the recommended clause.

The preparation of income tax returns is a seasonal affair and under the pressure of meeting a filing deadline, the tax preparer often does not have sufficient time to render tax-planning advice. In a legal checkup, an attorney can render tax-planning advice, and often in reviewing past income tax returns, he can discover a possible tax refund claim.

If you are engaged in a business, an attorney can render valuable advice on the best form of business organization for you and on many subjects relating to the conduct of your business, including, for example, group health and pension and profit-sharing plans.

If you have not had a legal checkup recently, you have overlooked an impressive opportunity for the more effective management, preservation, and disposition of your property at the least possible tax cost.

chapter 16

EXECUTE A POWER OF ATTORNEY AND A LIVING WILL

A power of attorney is a written instrument by which you, as principal, appoint an attorney-in-fact to act as your agent and confer upon him the authority to act in your behalf. A power of attorney may be either general (giving your attorney-in-fact power to do almost anything on your behalf) or special (giving your attorney-in-fact only the power to do one or more specific things). Death cancels a power of attorney, and you can call it off at any time during your life. You may appoint one person as your attorney-in-fact and also appoint a successor to act in the event of the death or disability of your original appointee.

You should grant a power of attorney to someone although you may retain the power of letting it be delivered only when your appointee needs to act in your behalf. For example, you may grant a power of attorney to your wife (husband), your brother (sister), your son (daughter), or a business associate, leaving the power with your attorney to be delivered to the appointee only in the event that your attorney-in-fact needs to act.

If you should have a heart attack, someone should be authorized to sign checks to pay bills, borrow money if necessary, and file insurance claims. If you plan to be away from home for two weeks or longer on a vacation or a business trip, something might arise in your absence which should be dealt with immediately. Your return home could be delayed and someone would need an authorization to file an income tax return for you or to obtain an extension of time until you return. Later on in life, you may have the misfortune of becoming senile or weak and disabled. Here again, someone should have the authority to take care of your business for you.

In some jurisdictions, incompetency terminates a power of attorney. If you should live in one of those, you may wish to create a revocable living trust while you are possessed of your senses. After all, anyone who lives long enough may suffer cerebral arteriosclerosis or otherwise through senility be unable to manage his affairs.

Powers of attorney should not, of course, be handed out indiscriminately. There is always the risk of abuse. Ordinarily, this can be avoided by leaving a power of attorney with your attorney or your banker to be delivered only if in his judgment circumstances are such that you would want it to become effective. A sample general power of attorney is provided in Appendix H.

You may also wish to consider executing a living will. Today with intravenous feedings, heart-lung machines, and other devices, a patient who has no chance whatsoever of survival can be kept alive by artificial means. If you do not want this to happen to you, then execute a living will such as this one:

> To my family, my physician, my lawyer, my clergyman:
> To any medical facility in whose care I happen to be:
> To any individual who may become responsible for my health, welfare or affairs:
>
> Death is as much a reality as birth, growth, maturity, and old age. It is the only certainty of life. If the time comes when I can no longer take part in decisions for my own future, let this statement stand as an expression of my wishes while I am still of sound mind.
>
> If the situation should arise in which there is no reasonable expectation of my recovery from physical or mental disability, I request that I be allowed to die and not be kept alive by artificial means or "heroic measures." I do not fear death itself as much as the indignities of deterioration, dependence, and hopeless pain. I therefore ask that medication be mercifully administered to me to alleviate suffering even though this may hasten the moment of death.

If I have executed a valid form of bequeathal of any of my organs for transplant or other purposes, I do, however, authorize and request that I be kept alive by artificial means for a time sufficient to enable a physician or physicians to harvest after my death the organ or organs to be transplanted.

This request is made after careful consideration. I hope you who care for me will feel morally bound to follow its mandate. I recognize that this appears to place a heavy responsibility upon you, but it is with the intention of relieving you of such responsibility and of placing it upon myself in accordance with my strong convictions that this statement is made.

_____

_____
Date

_____
Witness

_____
Witness

As yet there are only a few states in which the legislative enactments have recognized the right of the individual to let himself die, let alone the right of another to make that decision for him. Nevertheless, a living will delivered to your family, your physician, your clergyman, and your attorney may persuade them to honor your wishes.

You may also wish to consider leaving your eyes, your kidneys, your heart, some other part or all of your body to make life possible and meaningful for someone who is on a waiting list praying for his vision or his life. Your entire body is also needed for research and educational purposes.

In over 20 states, legislation requires provision on an automobile driver's license for a space in which the driver may indicate whether or not he wishes to make an anatomical gift, to take effect upon his death. The National Kidney Foundation, 116 East 27th Street, New York, New York 10016, also has available a form of bequeathal which does not name a specific recipient and which is legally valid in all 50 states. If you bequeath all or part of your body for scientific and educational purposes, you should ask your family physician and members of your family to notify the proper medical institution by telephone immediately after your death.

Life and happiness for someone else is the most meaningful gift that you or anyone else can make.

chapter 17

NEGOTIATE A CUSTODY CONTRACT

If you and your wife should die in a common disaster, who would get the custody of your minor children? If you are divorced and have custody of your children, who will take your place if you should die? If you are a widow or a widower with a minor child or children, who will raise them for you if you should die before they become of age?

By a will you can dispose of your property and of your body. You can appoint a trustee to manage your estate and to distribute income and principal for the support, education, and maintenance of your children. You may request, but you cannot compel, someone to accept custody and to raise them for you. What can you do?

First, if you are married, you and your wife should make a decision, to be reviewed periodically, as to whom you would like to take over your parental responsibilities. Maybe your parents or hers could and would accept the children. Another possibility, and often a better one because of the age factor, is a brother, a sister, a brother-in-law, or a sister-in-law. If one of these should have children of approximately the same age, you might be able to enter into a mutual agreement under which they would assume the custody of your children or alternatively you would serve as a custodian of their children if either set of parents should die leaving minor children to survive.

Later, if you have an older child who marries, then you might want to change the custody arrangement to let that child take care of his or her younger brothers and sisters. Occasionally, if you do not have anyone in your family or your wife's family who could and would take over for you, there is always the possibility of your having a good and capable friend who, confronted with the same risk, would enter into a mutual custody arrangement.

You cannot, of course, expect anyone to assume the financial responsibility of raising your children, and your estate plan should be designed to create through insurance and savings funds sufficient to support, educate, and maintain your children until they are of age. Social security benefits will not cover the total cost, but you can always supplement your estate by renewable term insurance to be carried in large amounts as long as you have minor children to support.

If you do not have a custody agreement, no one may volunteer, or a dispute could develop between your family and your wife's family over who should take the children. The problem could be more serious if you are divorced and do not believe that your former spouse would be a fit and proper person to have custody of your children. Admittedly, you cannot prevent him or her from trying simply by writing a contract with someone else, but all children are wards of the court, and the existence of a contract would be a factor in awarding the custody of minor children.

Your children are your most important assets. Do not forget about them when you do your estate planning.

chapter 18

WRITE A LETTER
TO YOUR EXECUTOR-TRUSTEE

Your executor-trustee is going to need all the information that you have assembled for your attorney and more. After all, he is going to take your place in carrying on your business, managing your investments, and making financial provision for your family. With your will, you should have a current balance sheet, all of your life insurance policies, partnership agreements, stockholders agreements, pension plans, profit-sharing plans, stock options, and deferred compensation agreements. Do not forget to revise the balance sheet regularly, preferably every year.

If you own an interest in a closely held business, the disposition of which is not controlled by a buy-and-sell agreement, by all means tell your executor whether you want the business retained or sold. If it is to be kept in your estate, your executor will need your advice as to which of your key employees can run it or as to how to find a competent manager. If it is to be sold, you will know far more than your executor about how the business should be valued and where to locate prospective purchasers.

If your will gives discretionary power to your executor-trustee in the distribution of income and principal, he will need complete and specific information about your family. For example, to illustrate the detailed information which you should give him, you might want to say in one letter that you have given a child a car upon graduation from college or upon marriage and that you want each other child to be given a car at that same stage in life. You might want to point out that you have paid for an expensive wedding and reception for one daughter and that your other daughter should have the same things done for her.

Your letter or letters are not to be mailed during your lifetime but are to be left with your will for delivery only to your executor at your death. You can change the letters from time to time as circumstances require.

If your wife cannot balance a checkbook, ask your executor to aid her in the management of her own financial affairs. If you have a child who is a spendthrift, warn your executor to be careful and prudent in distributions to him or her.

If you have a son or daughter whose marriage is in jeopardy, be frank with your executor about that. If you have a son or a son-in-law who could never make a success of a business venture, tell your executor never to make a loan for that purpose.

If your will authorizes your trustee to make distributions to your wife for her support and maintenance after considering other sources of income and support which she may from time to time have, explain to your trustee exactly what you mean. Tell him, for example, that if your widow remarries, you certainly do not want to support a second husband. On the other hand, if he, too, should die or become totally disabled, ask your executor to begin again making distributions to your widow. After all, you would not want her starving while your children are well provided for.

There are many things about your family that you would not want to include in a will, which is to be recorded in the courthouse. Then, too, over the years your children, their spouses, and your grandchildren will mature. You will view them differently with each passing year, and your changing attitudes should be reflected in letter revisions as required.

In writing letters to your executor to be kept with your will, your objective should be to keep him currently advised of everything which he could conceivably need to know about your assets, your liabilities, and the members of your family. With your advice, he can do a much better job of taking your place.

chapter 19

CHECK YOUR ESTATE PLAN CAREFULLY

After your attorney has completed a first draft of your entire estate plan and before you sign anything, check every document carefully. First, and above all, make sure that your property is to be distributed according to your wishes and instructions. After all, the primary purpose of a living trust, a will, life insurance endorsements, and pension and profit-sharing designations is to protect and provide for those for whom you care. Second, make sure this primary objective has been accomplished at the least possible tax cost. Has advantage been taken of the marital deduction if it is needed? Will your property continue to pass under your will for more than one generation?

Next, review the administrative provisions to make certain that your executor-trustee has been given adequate power to act without having to seek the advice and consent of a probate court. Paper is cheaper than lawsuits. Do not risk appointing a well-chosen executor-trustee who cannot perform adequately because you have failed to give him authority to act.

In reading your will, you may come across some words which are not in your everyday vocabulary. The phrases *per capita* and *per stirpes* may be among these. If the words *per stirpes* are used, then the children of a deceased child will receive their parent's share. The words *per capita* require an equal division to each person irrespective of relationship. A diagram may help you understand the words better.

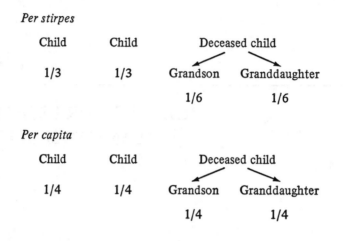

Per stirpes

Child	Child	Deceased child
1/3	1/3	Grandson Granddaughter
		1/6 1/6

Per capita

Child	Child	Deceased child
1/4	1/4	Grandson Granddaughter
		1/4 1/4

Occasionally, a grandfather or a grandmother will want a division among grandchildren on a per capita rather than a per stirpes basis, but this sometimes creates two problems. First, each child as distinguished from the grandchildren usually believes that a distribution should be on a per stirpes basis. Second, if a per capita distribution is used, the will or trust agreement must contain a provision stating the time at which the class closes. The common law incorrectly assumes that people can continue to have children as long as they live, and therefore the members of a class composed of grandchildren could not be determined until the date of death of the last of your own children. This difficulty can be met by stating a year or an event upon which a class will close and beyond which no further members of the class will be admitted.

So far, we have discussed only the basic provisions of a will: (1) the appointment of an executor, (2) the distribution of property, and (3) administrative provisions. A well-drafted will covers far more than that.

Most wills direct an executor to pay just debts and funeral expenses, but an executor would take care of these responsibilities anyhow. You may wish, however, to direct your executor to have a monument or a marker erected at your grave, and you should certainly be more precise about the payment of debts. For example, is a loan on a life insurance policy to be paid out of the policy proceeds? Is the mortgage on a home, a rental property, a car, or some other asset to be paid out of that particular property or with the proceeds from some other asset of your estate.

Preferably, every will should contain a provision concerning the payment of death taxes. U.S. estate taxes are imposed against your estate and must be paid by your executor out of the assets of your estate. In the final distribution, however, who should bear the burden of these taxes? Should the U.S. estate taxes be treated as if the assessment constituted a debt of your estate, or should the beneficiaries of your estate in effect bear a proportionate part of those taxes depending on what each receives?

State inheritance taxes generally are imposed not upon the right to give but upon the right to receive. The executor has an obligation to pay these taxes, but, in most states, he is required to charge the state inheritance taxes to the particular beneficiaries. Here again, is that what you want, or do you prefer that state inheritance taxes also be treated as if these constituted a debt of your estate? If any death taxes must be paid out of the property left to your wife outright or in trust to obtain the marital deduction, then you will not obtain the full advantage of the marital deduction under your will. The will in Appendix A contains one kind of a tax clause which can be used in a marital deduction with an estate of $1,200,000 or less. In larger estates it is often wiser to let a portion of the taxes be paid out of the marital trust. For example, in 1982 in an adjusted gross estate of $6,000,000 with one half being placed in the marital trust and one half in a family trust the U.S. estate tax alone will be $1,228,000. If all taxes were payble out of the family trust, there would have been left after the U.S. estate tax alone only $1,772,000 in the family trust as compared with $3,000,000 in the marital trust. A provision for the payment of death taxes should not be inadvertently and accidentally made part of the clause creating a marital deduction formula.

In all probability, your will should have a common disaster clause. It is possible that you and your wife might die in an accident so that it would be difficult if not impossible to determine which of you died first. In most states, under the Uniform Simultaneous Death Act or a similar statutory provision, you may declare in your will that your wife shall be deemed to survive. This declaration will give you the benefit of the marital deduction even though a coroner might be in doubt as to which death occurred first. Second, in states imposing an inheritance tax and granting exemptions based on relationship, the state death tax would also be less if your wife were presumed to have survived you. Conceivably, of course, for nontax reasons, you might prefer instead a presumption that you survived your wife.

Next, make sure that your will does not violate the rule against perpetuities. Under this rule, a fee simple interest or absolute title must vest not later than 21 years after any reasonable number of lives in being at the time of the creation of the interest. For example, you cannot create a valid trust for grandchildren until each has reached the age of 25 unless your will provides that the trust, in any event, will come to an end 21 years after the death of the last of your descendents living on the date of your death. A rule against perpetuities clause appears as Article VII in the model will in Appendix A.

If yours is a marital deduction will, make certain that it includes two valuable techniques for avoiding overutilization of the marital deduction. First, the following clause or its equivalent should be added to any language utilized for creating a formula for devise and bequest:

> provided, however, that the amount placed in the marital trust shall be reduced by a sum sufficient for this estate to make full use of the unified estate and gift tax credit and the credit for state death taxes.

An example will illustrate the value of the clause. In 1987, the new unified tax credit will be $192,800. This means that a husband and wife may then shelter $1,200,000 between them plus a credit allowed for state death taxes against the federal estate tax. If the husband, however, used the maximum marital deduction by leaving his entire estate to his wife, no federal tax whatsoever would be imposed, but his wife's estate would suffer a tax of $235,000 (before a credit for state death taxes) assuming that she died with an adjusted gross estate of $1,200,000.

The full use of the marital deduction may be detrimental rather than beneficial. Furthermore, there is always the possibility that the surviving spouse may have an estate of his or her own acquired either before or after the death of the testator.

Fortunately, there is another escape from overutilization of the marital deduction. The Tax Reform Act of 1976 provides a new set of rules for disclaimers. To be effective, a qualified disclaimer must constitute an irrevocable and unqualified refusal to accept an interest in property and it must satisfy four requirements: (1) the refusal must be in writing; (2) it must be received by the transferor, the legal representative of the transferor, or the holder of title to the property not later than nine months after the day on which the transfer is made; (3) the person executing the disclaimer must not have accepted the interest or any of its benefits; and (4) the disclaimed interest must pass to someone other than the person making the disclaimer without any direction on the part of the person making the disclaimer. Under the Revenue Act of 1978, the disclaimer will not be disqualified because it results in the property still passing to the surviving spouse who disclaimed it, for example, to a trust in which the surviving spouse is entitled to an income interest. As a protective device, the following article should be added to all marital deduction wills:

> Each beneficiary under this will shall have the right to disclaim in whole or in part any devise or bequest by delivering a written statement of disclaimer to the executor within nine months after the date of my death. Any portion of the marital trust which is disclaimed shall become a part of the family trust, and any portion of the family trust which is disclaimed shall become a part of the marital trust.

In most states, the statutes require the probate court to appoint appraisers, and the executor is under a duty to see that an appraisal is made and to file settlements with the court periodically. These statutes were adopted primarily for the protection of creditors, and in a solvent estate with an executor of integrity, these are unnecessary expenses which can in some states be avoided by a provision in a will relieving the executor from the duty of obtaining an appraisal and for the responsibility of filing settlements. In practice, settlements are not audited by many courts, and your family will be better protected by a requirement that an annual accounting be made to each current income beneficiary who shall have, perhaps, 60 days within which to make an objection.

After you have approved and signed your will, ask for a copy of it which you may take home with you. The original should be placed in your lockbox or in your attorney's lockbox, and you should never write anything on the original. If at some time you want changes made in your will, make notations on your copy and take that to your attorney. Words inserted on an executed will can invalidate the will.

chapter 20

REVIEW YOUR ESTATE PLAN REGULARLY

Ask your attorney to review your will whenever there is a change in either state or federal tax law that might affect your estate planning. Some members of the bar keep on file cards an abstract of each will in the office so that this service can be performed for every client quickly and economically.

But your attorney cannot possibly know of all of the things that may happen in your life. If any of the following events occur, you should review the potential effect on your estate planning to determine whether your will or trust should be amended or revised in its entirety:

1. Marriage.
2. Divorce.
3. Adoption of a child.
4. Birth of a child.
5. Death of a child.
6. Birth of a grandchild.
7. Death of a grandchild.
8. Marriage of a child.
9. Divorce of a child.
10. Death of a spouse.

11. Increase in personal wealth.
12. Decrease in personal wealth.
13. Receipt of substantial inheritance or gift.
14. Making of a substantial gift.
15. Purchase of life insurance.
16. Participating in a new pension or profit-sharing plan.
17. Move to another state.
18. Special circumstances relating to a child, e.g., special needs such as education, health, or business.

In many states, either marriage or divorce invalidates any existing will. Some states permit the execution of a will in anticipation of marriage, but the will must specifically cite that fact. In any event, either marriage or divorce will drastically change your testamentary plans.

In a divorce proceeding, alimony payable under the court's decree or under a written agreement incident to the divorce may or may not be taxable income to the wife and deductible by the husband. Furthermore, whenever there is a property settlement as a part of a divorce proceeding, a transfer of assets which have appreciated in value may be a taxable capital gain. Payments for support of children may or may not be deductible by the husband, again depending in part upon the divorce decree or the support agreement.

If you or any one of your descendants should adopt a child, the question of whether or not that child can take under your will can best be resolved by a codicil to your will or by a total revision of your will. Obviously, the birth or the death of a child or a grandchild could affect your estate planning. Certainly your will should again be reviewed. The marriage of a child or the divorce of a child could also necessitate a revision in your estate plan.

If your wife dies, your will should be reviewed immediately. For example, a marital deduction will can no longer serve to reduce taxes, and without a wife to support, you may find it advisable to accelerate a program of gifts to your children. If, after the death of your wife, you should decide to remarry, not only will you need a new estate plan but preferably that estate plan should embrace a prenuptial agreement. When each party to the remarriage has children by a prior marriage, family difficulties may be minimized by property agreements made in advance of the marriage.

A substantial change in your personal wealth might also prompt a change in a program of giving to children and a revision in your will or trust to take advantage of an alternate approach for the reduction of taxes. Of course, if you receive a substantial inheritance or gift, or make a major gift to someone, once more your estate plan should be reviewed. Such increase or decrease could constitute a substantial change in your net worth, which might call for a total revision of your estate plan.

If you move to another state, you will encounter a different set of laws which will be applicable if you should die without a will, and in all probability if your wife should renounce your will in the other state, a different consequence would ensue. State laws also affect the type of administrative powers which you should be granted and the impact of state death taxes upon your estate plan. It is also more economical to probate a will if the witnesses to the will live in the same state in which you reside.

In every family, special circumstances develop from time to time that require the revision of an estate plan. The decision to attend graduate school, the disability of a member of the family, or a business success or reverse could make it advisable for you to review and revise your estate plan.

A will speaks of the moment of your death, and it should be kept current with the changes in your property ownerships, with your family relationships, and with the state and federal tax laws.

An act of Congress, a statute adopted in your home state, or a judicial decision may have a disastrous effect upon a well-designed estate plan. Such events occur so frequently that you should not discredit the attorney whom you consulted because his conclusions differ from the recommendations made here, nor should your family be disgusted with him if the rules change and you have failed to have your will reviewed.

chapter 21

SUPPORT A CHARITY

Substantial tax savings can be realized by making major charitable gifts in the form of appreciated property rather than cash. For example, if a taxpayer owns stock which has a market value of $1,000 but which cost him only $100, there will be a capital gain tax if the stock is sold. If the taxpayer is in a 50 percent bracket, the tax will be $180 (20 percent of the $900 gain). Consequently, for the taxpayer in a 50 percent tax bracket, the value of a $1,000 gift in cash is a tax deduction of $500, but a gift of appreciated property in this

Gift in cash		
Gift	$1,000	
Charitable deduction		
(50 percent of $1,000)	500	
Net cost		$500
Gift in kind		
Gift	$1,000	
Charitable deduction	$500	
Capital gain tax avoided	180	
Total		680
Net cost		$320

illustration would result in a charitable deduction of the value of $500 plus and a $180 savings in capital gain tax, making the net cost of the $1,000 gift in kind only $320.

On top of that, the gift has removed an asset from the taxpayer's estate which would be subject to death taxes if the gift were not made. The net result is that in this topsy-turvy world of taxes, you actually make money by giving money away. Furthermore, a life-time charitable gift affords the donor the pleasure of seeing the fruits of his generosity enjoyed by the charitable institution and prevents the accumulation of an additional estate through income that would be derived from the gift if the property were retained and added to the estate to be taxed at death.

Regrettably, gift tax laws have become encrusted with complexities. A comprehensive analysis is beyond the scope of this limited estate-planning survey, but at the risk of misleading by not including all of the exceptions and reservations, something must be said about the attractive alternatives that are available.

Under the Tax Reform Act of 1969, contributions made to certain charities may now be deducted up to 50 percent of adjusted gross income after disregarding any net operating loss. For most tax-payers, this means, simply, that they can deduct as contributions one half of their income before they have reduced it by exemptions and itemized deductions. The 50 percent limitation applies to contributions to religious groups, schools, hospitals, government units, and certain other organizations such as the Red Cross, community chest or fund, public museums, and libraries. Contributions to certain other charities, and this does not concern the average taxpayer, are subject to a 20 percent limitation. Gifts in excess of the limitations may be carried over and deducted in later tax years.

Every taxpayer who makes a gift of appreciated property gets a tax deduction, but the entire gift may not be deductible that year. Any gift of appreciated property is subject to a 30 percent rather than a 50 percent maximum unless the individual elects, as he should, to carry the excess over to later tax years.

For most of the contributions which you make during your life-time, you need to know only that you will realize a tax benefit by giving appreciated property rather than cash and that there will be a 30 percent limitation if you use appreciated property but that the excess above this can be carried over and deducted in later years.

If you give paintings, works of art, or other tangible (touchable) personal property to a qualified charity, your deduction will be reduced by 40 percent of your long-term capital gain unless the donee is able to use the property in a way related to its exempt purpose or function. For example, a gift of a painting to an art museum would not have to be reduced by 40 percent of the capital gain applicable if a sale had occurred.

Another interesting exception is that if you give "ordinary income property" to a charity, the deduction will be limited to your cost basis. Ordinary income property is property which if sold by you would result in ordinary income or a short-term capital gain. Inventory, crops raised, or livestock produced would come within this classification.

Private educational institutions are primarily dependent upon contributions for their survival. Our basic liberties will be threatened if the entire educational system is state owned. A free interchange of ideas can be assured only if we support and maintain our private colleges and universities. There are a number of ways in which you can make gifts to these and other organized charities and obtain at the same time tangible tax benefits.

First, you can reserve a life estate in a personal residence or a farm, giving the remainder to a charity upon your death. Under a special rule for valuing a deductible remainder interest in a personal residence or farm, you will be entitled to a significant charitable deduction on your income tax return.

Next, as an alternative, you can create a charitable remainder trust. Essentially, this action consists only of an arrangement with a charity under which it pays income to you or to you and your wife on the amount of your gift as long as you live, with the gift then belonging to the charity. You do not need to learn all of the rules about charitable remainder trusts because any charitable organization will be glad to furnish you all of the necessary forms and explanations. There are, however, three varieties of charitable remainder trusts and a brief explanation will show you some of the advantages of each.

An annuity trust provides for the payment of 5 percent or more of the fair market value of the property placed in trust. A unitrust provides for the payment of 5 percent or more of the net fair market value of the trust assets, valued annually. In other words, whereas the annuity trust provides a percentage on the initial fair market value, the unitrust provides for a percentage of the fluctuating market value. The third type of charitable remainder trust is a pooled income fund. Essentially, this is a trust administered by the charitable organization with the trustee making investments of contributed property in a diversified portfolio of securities which resembles in some respects a mutual fund. A subscriber to a pooled income fund receives income earned by the fund during one or more lives with the property thereafter going to the charitable organization.

The pooled income fund has the broadest appeal. If you purchase an interest by the use of appreciated stock or real estate, you do not incur any capital gain tax upon the transaction, but your charitable deduction would be determined on the basis of the market value of the securities transferred. The tax-deductible portion of a pooled income fund is a higher percentage of the total gift value than any other life income plan. For example, if you are aged 60 and your wife aged 58, the deductible portion of a $10,000 pooled income investment would be about $3,250.

If you have $10,000 or more in highly appreciated property and want to increase your income, you could trade your property to the charity for a high-income unitrust which would pay out the net income earned by the trust assets but not more than a stated percentage of the market value of those assets as valued each year. In the present market, an organized charity can invest in high-quality bonds yielding 14 percent or more. The income would be taxable to you as ordinary income. For example, if you gave $20,000 in stock which had a cost to you of $12,000, the charity would sell the stock and invest the proceeds in high-quality bonds with a net yield of 14 percent or better. Assuming that you or your wife are aged 60 and 58, respectively, you would get a tax deduction of about $1,047. You would not have a capital gain on the sale of the stock. The annual income from the donated assets might jump, for example, from $400 (2 percent on market value) to $2,800 (14 percent of $20,000). The contribution would also remove the entire gift from federal taxation at your death.

For the higher-bracket taxpayer, there are still more interesting possibilities. If you are interested in tax-free income, you can transfer to the charity property which has neither appreciated nor depreciated in value in exchange for a tax-exempt unitrust. The charitable organization would sell your gift and invest the contribution in tax-exempt bonds which might yield 6 percent or more. If you are in a 50 percent income tax bracket, 6 percent tax-exempt income is equal to almost 12 percent of ordinary income. At the lower yield of 6 percent, your tax deduction for the contribution will be larger than under some other unitrust plans. If you and your wife are aged 60 and 58 respectively, the deductible portion of a $10,000 gift would be $3,000. Once again, upon your death the existence of the trust would increase the tax-free marital deduction share of your estate to your wife, and only her remaining interest in the life income trust would be taxable. The contribution would effectively remove the balance of the gift from taxation at your death.

If you are a high-bracket taxpayer with $50,000 or more in highly appreciated stock or real estate, you might trade it to a charity for a straight unitrust. Your charitable deduction will be computed on the market value of the contribution, but you will not have to pay the capital gains tax. When the property is sold by the charity, the capital gain will not be taxable immediately either to you or to it, but if some of the gain is later paid out to you to meet the required yield of your contract, that portion of the payment will be reported by you as long-term capital gain rather than as ordinary income. In this type of unitrust, the charity ordinarily will keep your contribution invested in growth stocks which characteristically have a low dividend yield. This serves two purposes. With little ordinary income to distribute, most of the yield to you will be long-term capital gain. Second, investment in growth stocks makes it likely that the market value of the trust assets will increase, which also increases the amount payable to you. Most charities will guarantee to pay you 6 percent of the market value of the assets each year. In making this payment, the charity will first distribute ordinary income (such as dividends and interest), then realized long-term capital gain, and finally, if necessary, return of principal. You will carry each type of distribution through to your own tax return.

For example, if your gift is $50,000 in stock which cost you $20,000, the trust will pay you 6 percent of the market value of the assets each year and invest the proceeds in growth stocks yielding perhaps 1 percent on market value. If you are 60 and your wife is 58, and if you are both to be beneficiaries, the tax deduction will be $12,000. Income in the first full year will be $3,000 (6 percent of $50,000), consisting of $500 ordinary income and $2,500 long-term capital gain. If the trust grows 4 percent in the second year to $52,000, the yield in that year would be $520 ordinary income and $2,600 capital gain. If the assets continue to grow at a rate of 4 percent a year (after the annual yield to the beneficiary), their value would be about $65,000 in the seventh year, and the income to the

chapter 22

DON'T DIE INTESTATE

To die intestate is to die without a will. Almost everyone who owns any property entirely in his own name needs a will, and yet one sampling survey reports that only 19 percent of the total voting-age population have wills.

If you have a will, you can appoint an executor to settle your estate. If you die without one, the court will appoint an administrator to serve instead. In most states, a statute establishes an order of preference, but disputes often develop among children as to which one of them shall serve. You should exercise your right to select the person to settle your estate.

Every administrator appointed by a court must give bond with surety thereon to guarantee performance of his duties, and if there are minor children, a guardian must be qualified for each, and, again, a bond must be posted. This additional trouble and extra expense far exceeds the cost of drafting most wills.

The powers of the administrator, derived from statute, are seldom adequate to permit settlement of your estate efficiently and economically. In most states, securities cannot be sold without first incurring the expense of obtaining a court order.

If you die without a will, your real estate will go by statute to your heirs and not to your administrator. If there are minors involved, the real estate cannot be sold without a court order, and if all of your heirs are of age, all of them must agree upon the operation or sale of your real estate assets.

The greatest danger of dying without a will is that the laws of your state will determine how your property is to be divided, and that division will seldom be exactly what you would want. For example, in some states, if you die without a will, one half of your property will go to your spouse and one half to your children. If you have a small estate, you would probably prefer that your entire estate go to your wife, and certainly you would not want any of it to go to minor children whose rights would be dependent upon the qualification of a guardian.

In other states, the statute might provide that one half of your personal property would go to your spouse and one half to your children, with your spouse having, however, only one third interest for life in the real estate. This division of realty is totally impractical.

Typically, if a person dies without leaving a spouse or a descendant to survive him, one half of his estate will go to his mother and one half to his father, but if either of them has died, then the entirety will go to the survivor. Often this results in death taxes being imposed upon property distributed to aged parents with the tax being assessed again when the parents die and leave the property to their other children.

In a few states, the Uniform Probate Code has been adopted. It is far better than most intestacy laws but far from perfect. No one can design a uniform house which would be suitable for every family in the United States, and yet that is what every law of intestacy attempts to do with property: to make the same distribution no matter what the situation.

Under the Uniform Probate Code, your property would pass to your wife if you had neither issue nor parents surviving. If you should die with issue of your marriage to your surviving spouse, the first $50,000 plus one half of the balance would go to her and the other half to the issue. If there are issue but one or more of them are not also issue of the surviving spouse, then your estate would go equally to your surviving spouse and to all of the issue without the first $50,000 passing to your surviving spouse.

The Uniform Probate Code and other laws of intestacy cover all of the other possible variations including death without leaving a spouse, issue, parent, brother, or sister to survive. Some states give adopted children the same rights of inheritance as natural children.

Some states give a preference to relatives of the whole blood over relatives of the half blood. There is an enormous variation in the treatment of illegitimate children.

"Only the wealthy need wills" is a false saying which overlooks the fact that the less property you have, the more important it becomes to distribute that property properly. The assets of a multi-millionaire will take care of all his loved ones no matter how the assets are divided by statute. Furthermore, only by careful estate planning can you be assured that your property will be distributed to those whom you love at the least possible tax cost.

in Article VI, all estate, inheritance, transfer and succession taxes payable by my estate or payable on the legacies given herein, and my Executor shall make no claims against any person receiving any money or property including the proceeds of insurance policies includable in my gross estate for death tax purposes on account of such taxes being assessed because of such money or property.

ARTICLE III. I hereby declare that all of the household and homestead furniture and furnishings of every kind and character, including (but without being limited to) furniture, rugs, silver, china-ware, linens, paintings and all other similar articles which have been utilized by my wife and me in our home belong to and are the exclusive property of my wife.

ARTICLE IV. I bequeath all of my personal letters, jewelry, automobiles, personal effects and clothing to my wife if she be living on the date of my death, but if she predecease me, then to my children equally, *per stirpes*.

MARITAL TRUST

ARTICLE V. If my wife survives me, I devise and bequeath to my Trustee to be held as part of the marital trust that fractional share of my residuary estate which, when added to all other property included in the amount determined and allowed as a marital deduction in the computation of United States estate taxes assessed in my estate, shall be equal to one-half of my adjusted gross estate as de fined under the Internal Revenue Code, provided, however, that the amount placed in the marital trust shall be reduced by a sum sufficient for this estate to make full use of the unified estate and gift tax credit and the credit for state death taxes. The calculation is to be made as if death taxes are not payable out of the marital share. The values to be used for the purpose of computing the fractional share shall be those values finally established in the United States tax proceeding, provided, however, that the trust estate to be divided pursuant to this provision shall not embrace and include the proceeds of life insurance, the proceeds of profit sharing plans, or any other properties which by designation of beneficiary or otherwise may be made payable to the Trustee for the use and benefit only of either the Marital Trust or the Family trusts. Any property distributed to the Trustee in kind shall be allocated in the lower of (1) its value at the time of distribution and (2) its value as finally determined for United States estate tax purposes, provided, however, that if a beneficiary of my estate shall be Executor-Trustee thereof, the selection of the property to be allocated to this trust shall not be made by the Executor-Trustee but by that institution next eligible to qualify as Executor-Trustee under this will. Subject to the foregoing, the Executor or the successor, as the case may be, shall have absolute discretion in selecting the property to be allocated pursuant to this provision without any duty to make a ratable apportionment of values, provided, however, that the assets selected and transferred must qualify for the marital deduction. This portion of my estate shall be held in trust upon the following terms, provisions, and conditions for the following uses and purposes.

Section A. Commencing with the date of my death, my Trustee shall pay to my beloved wife quarterly or oftener if she shall request it, all of the income of this trust during her life, and upon her death, my Trustee shall have the right to pay out of the income or principal of this trust, the funeral expenses for my wife.

Section B. In addition to the net income, my Trustee in the exercise of its uncontrolled discretion shall pay to my wife as much of the principal of this trust as my Trustee shall deem needful or desirable for her comfortable support and maintenance including medical, surgical, hospital or other institutional care so that my wife shall receive income and principal sufficient to maintain her station in life and the standard of living that she is enjoying at the date of my death.

Section C. Without reference to whether or not my wife survives me, my Trustee shall pay principal and any undistributed income of this trust unto such persons and in such estates, interests, and proportions as my wife by will shall appoint, provided, however, that any appointment must make specific reference to this power. In all other respects, my wife, in the exercise of this power of appointment, shall not be limited in any manner but, in all respects, the power shall be general and absolute and shall include specifically the power in my wife to appoint to her estate. If my wife shall fail to exercise the power of appointment herein granted as to any property in this trust, then upon her death (whether before or after my death), the Trustee shall pay to the Executor or Administrator of my wife's estate any income of this trust which is accrued, undistributed, and not appointed by her plus whatever amount from the principal not effectively appointed as is requested in writing by her Executor or Administrator within twelve (12) months after her death but not exceeding the total amount of the federal and state death taxes and interest thereon, if any, payable by her estate by reason of the inclusion in her estate of the assets remaining in this trust. All of the property remaining in this trust shall be poured over into and become a part of the Family Trust hereinafter created.

Section D. In the administration of this trust, my Trustee shall have and exercise all the rights and powers hereinafter granted to my

Trustee provided only that there shall be, and there is hereby, excepted and excluded therefrom any and all of the powers hereinafter created which might or could cause or result in a loss of the marital deduction under the federal estate tax law; and provided further that this trust shall be administered separately and apart from the trusts hereinafter created unless my wife shall request that, for the purposes of administration only, the trusts created by this will be combined; and further provided that this request shall not be honored if, by reason of a joint administration of the various trusts herein created, the marital deduction provided for in the federal estate tax law shall be lost or forfeited.

Section E. If there is no sufficient evidence as to the order of our deaths, my wife shall be presumed to have survived me and this will shall be construed upon that assumption and basis.

FAMILY TRUST

ARTICLE VI. I specifically refrain from exercising any power of appointment which I may have under any will, contract, trust agreement, profit sharing agreement or otherwise, and I devise and bequeath all of my other property, real, personal, and mixed in which I have or I or my estate shall hereafter acquire any interest, present or future, vested or contingent, to my Trustee to hold in trust for a period no longer than the lives of my wife and my descendants living on the date of my death and twenty years and eleven months thereafter upon and for the following uses and purposes:

Section A. The property in this trust shall be deemed to consist of (a) all of the property originally in this trust and (b) all the property received from the marital trust created in Article V or from any other source, and my Trustee shall divide on a *per stirpes* basis the property in this trust (as thus calculated) into as many equal shares as I shall have children living ten months after my death, and children dead with issue surviving ten months after my death, and shall set up a separate trust for each child then living and one for the issue as a group of each deceased child, with each share being known as a "Child's Trust," and with the shares as a whole being identified as the "Family Trust," provided, however, that the shares of this trust may be held and administered together with the Trustee being under a duty only to make a separate accounting for and a separate income tax return for each of the separate shares or separate trusts.

Section B. The Trustee, out of the Family Trust, charging an equal portion to each Child's Trust, shall pay to my wife that portion of the income and principal thereof necessary to provide for her according to the standard of living that she is enjoying at the date of my death provided, however, that the Trustee shall not make any distribution of principal to my wife until she shall have exhausted all the income and principal of the marital trust and provided, further, that the Trustee in its discretion shall take into consideration the individual estate of my wife and any and all other sources of income and support which she may from time to time have.

Section C. If in any year all or any part of the income of the Family Trusts created by this Article shall not be paid to my wife, such income may be accumulated insofar as it may be lawfully accumulated and added to the principal of the trusts created by this Article or, alternatively, such income may be distributed in the manner provided by subsequent sections of this Article.

Section D. Provided only that a sufficient reserve of principal can be and is maintained for discharge of the benefits provided for my wife, the Trustee, out of the Family Trusts, charging an equal portion to each Child's Trust, shall pay each of my children income and principal sufficient for the maintenance and education of that child until that child has reached the age of twenty-three years.

Section E. Provided only that a sufficient reserve of principal can be and is maintained to provide for the protection and security of my wife under previous sections and articles of this will, my Trustee may pay each child that part of the income and principal of that Child's Trust necessary to supplement his or her earnings for his or her maintenance and support. My Trustee, out of a Child's Trust, may also advance a portion of the principal thereof to the beneficiary of that trust for the purpose of purchasing a home, or alternatively the Trustee may purchase a home as Trustee for the use and benefit of that child with the purchase to be made out of the principal of that Child's Trust and with the title to be held by the Trustee until such time as the Trustee deems it wise to place title in the name of that child. My Trustee, out of a Child's Trust, may lend a portion of the principal thereof to the beneficiary of that trust for any purpose deemed sufficient by my Trustee, with such loan, if any, to be made upon such terms and with such security, if any, as the Trustee may require.

Section F. Before making any loan or distribution of principal as otherwise authorized by Section E hereof, my Trustee shall be required to obtain from my wife, if living, advance approval of any proposed distribution of principal. Subject only to this limitation, absolute power is granted to my Trustee not only to relieve my Trustee from seeking judicial instruction, but to the extent that my Trustee deems it to be prudent, to make determinations freely in favor of liberal distributions to current income beneficiaries. In each instance, the rights of all subsequent beneficiaries shall be subordinate, but my Trustee shall not be answerable to any of the lifetime beneficiaries nor to any subsequent beneficiary for anything done or omitted in favor of a current income beneficiary; but no current income beneficiary shall have the right to compel any such favorable treatment.

Section G. Upon the death of my wife and upon the attainment of the age of twenty-three years of all of my children, my Trustee shall pay to each child at such time or times and in such amounts as the Trustee in its unlimited discretion shall deem such distribution to be in the best interest of such child the income and principal of that Child's Trust. The power granted to my Trustee to make and also to defer making a distribution, various partial distributions, and a final distribution of the principal of each Child's Trust shall not be subject to modification or interpretation by any court but shall be deemed as broadly discretionary as the power I might possess myself if living. Inasmuch as the needs of each of my children and their respective abilities to care for property shall differ, the Trustee is not only authorized but expected to follow, if advisable, a different pattern of distribution for each child.

Section H. If any of my children die before this trust terminates leaving widow, widower, descendants, spouses of descendants, or widow or widower of deceased descendants living at the date of said deceased child's death, my Trustee shall pay his or her share of the income and of the principal to his widow, her widower, and/or to such of his or her descendants, spouses of descendants, and widow or widower of deceased descendants as said child shall by will appoint, provided, however, that any daughter of mine shall not have the right to appoint to her widower or to any widower of any of her descendants anything other than an estate for life or until his remarriage, whichever shall sooner occur, and in the event of any such appointment, the Trustee may invade the principal of my estate for the benefit of the descendants of any daughter exercising the power of appointment without reference to the fact that such invasion of principal will diminish the life estate benefits.

Section I. If any of my children die before this trust terminates without having exercised the power of appointment provided for in Section H hereof, my Trustee shall distribute this child's trust to his or her children equally *per stirpes,* but if any of my children die before this trust terminates without leaving descendants at the date of said deceased child's death and without having exercised the power of appointment provided for in Section H hereof, my Trustee shall distribute this child's trust equally among the remaining trusts established for my family under this Article.

Section J. If pursuant to this will, a person under twenty-three years of age other than one of my children shall become entitled to a devise or bequest, such devise or bequest shall become and be impressed with a trust and held in trust by my Trustee until that particular person attains the age of twenty-three years, and I direct my Trustee to spend for each such person as much of the income and principal of that trust as is necessary for that person's education, maintenance and support until that person is twenty-three years of age; whereupon, my Trustee shall pay to that person the principal and any undistributed income of his or her trust.

Section K. If at any time or from time to time any beneficiary hereunder shall be under twenty-three years of age, the Trustee is to make payments in its sole discretion in any one or more of the following ways: (a) directly to such beneficiary, (b) directly in payment of the expense of support, maintenance, education and welfare of such beneficiary, (c) to the legal or natural guardian of such beneficiary, (d) or to any relative or guardian of the person of such beneficiary who shall have custody and care of the person of such beneficiary. The Trustee shall not be obligated to see to the application of the funds so paid, but the receipt of such payee shall be full acquittance to the Trustee, and all such distributions may be without the intervention of any guardian or any court, provided, however, that the Trustee in its discretion may require an accounting and take such steps as it may deem requisite to assure and enforce the due application of such money to the purpose for which it is intended.

Section L. Notwithstanding the foregoing provision of this Article VI, my wife shall have the right and the power to appoint the entirety of the income and principal of my estate to such of our descendants, spouses of descendants, and widow or widower of deceased descendants as my wife shall by deed or will appoint.

ARTICLE VII. Notwithstanding any other provision of this will, all of the property of my estate shall be finally distributed not later than twenty years and eleven months after the date of death of the last survivor of my descendants living on the date of my death and at the expiration of such period, if any part of my estate remains undistributed, the same shall immediately vest in and be distributed to the persons then entitled to receive the income from the trust estate in the proportions to which they are so entitled.

ARTICLE VIII. Each beneficiary and the personal representative of each beneficiary under this will shall have the right to disclaim in whole or in part any devise or bequest by delivering a written statement of disclaimer to the Executor within nine months after the date of my death. Any portion of the Marital Trust which is disclaimed shall become a part of the Family Trust, and any portion of the Family Trust which is disclaimed shall become a part of the Marital Trust.

ARTICLE IX. Certain of my life insurance policies may be made payable to my testamentary trustee, thereby exempting those proceeds from state inheritance taxes. My Trustee may lend all or any portion of these life insurance proceeds to my Executor.

ARTICLE X. My Executor shall not be required to file an inventory or appraisal with any court and neither my Executor nor my Trustee shall be required to make an accounting or to file any settlement with any court unless requested by a current income beneficiary of my estate. Within four months after the close of each fiscal year of my estate, the Executor or the Trustee thereof will render a written account of the administration of the trust estate to current income beneficiaries thereof. The written approval of such accounting by a majority of all current income beneficiaries (the parent, guardian, or conservator acting on behalf of any beneficiary who is a minor or otherwise incompetent) shall be final and binding as to all matters stated in said account or as shown thereby upon all persons (whether or not in being) who are then or thereafter may become eligible to share in either the principal or the income of my estate. The failure of any beneficiary to object in writing to the acting fiduciary to such an account within sixty days after the receipt of the same shall be final and binding to the same extent as if the written assent were given as hereinbefore provided.

ARTICLE XI. I empower my Executor, any successor Executor, my Trustee and any successor Trustee:

Section 1. To allot, assign, care for, collect, contract with respect to convey, convert, deal with, dispose of, enter into, exchange, hold, improve, insure, invest, lease, manage, mortgage, grant and exercise options with respect to, take possession of, pledge, protect, receive, release, repair, sell, sue for, and in general, to do any and every act and thing and to enter into and carry out any and every agreement with respect to the trust estate or any part thereof as the trustee would have the right to do if it were the individual owner thereof and as it may deem in the best interest of the beneficiaries of the trust, without being limited in any way by the grant of specific powers hereinafter made.

Section 2. To retain, without liability for loss or depreciation resulting from such retention, original property, real or personal, for such time as to it shall seem best, although such property may not be of the character prescribed by law or by the terms of this instrument for the investment of other trust funds and although it represents a large percentage of the total property of the trust estate; and to dispose of such original property by sale or exchange or otherwise as and when it shall deem advisable and receive and administer the proceeds as a part of the trust estate; and, if non-income-producing property is retained, then upon the sale, exchange or other disposition of such property, to make a reasonable apportionment of the proceeds between income and principal so as to make up for the loss of income during the period of retention of the unproductive property.

Section 3. To continue and operate any business which I may own or in which I may be financially interested at the time of my death, whether as sole proprietor, partner or shareholder for such time as it may deem to be for the best interest of my estate; to delegate such duties and the requisite powers to any employee, manager, or partner as it may deem proper without liability for such delegation except for its own negligence; to employ in the conduct of any such business, not only my capital investment therein at the time of my death, but also such additional capital out of my general estate as it may deem proper; to borrow money for any such business, either alone or along with other persons financially interested in the business, and to secure such loan or loans by a pledge or mortgage not only of my property or interest in the business, but also of any part of my property outside the business as my executor or trustee may deem proper; to lend money out of my estate or out of any trust hereby created to any business in which my estate or any trust hereby created is financially interested; to organize, either by itself or jointly with others, a corporation to carry on any business; to contribute all or any part of my interest in any business as capital to any such corporation; to accept stock in the corporation in lieu thereof and if it deems advisable to provide for different classes of stock and bonds; to sell any business and any interest in any business or any stock or other securities representing my interest in any business as and when and upon such terms as shall seem to it to be for the best interest of my estate; to liquidate, either by itself or jointly with others, any business or any interest in any business at such times and upon such terms as shall seem to be for the best interest of my estate; and generally, to exercise with respect to the continuance, management, sale or liquidation of any business interest I own at the time of my death, all the powers which I myself could have exercised during my lifetime.

Section 4. To invest and reinvest and keep the trust estate invested in any kind of property, real or personal, including by way of illustration, but not limitation, livestock, common and preferred stocks, voting trust certificates, bonds, notes, debentures, mortgages, shares or interest in investment trusts, shares or interest in common trust funds, investments that yield a high rate of income or no income at all, and wasting investments, without regard to the proportion any such investment or investments of a similar character may bear to the total trust estate or whether or not such investments are in new issues or in new or foreign enterprises, and without being limited to the classes of investments in which trustees are or may be authorized by statute or case or rule of court to invest trust funds, to buy and sell stocks, bonds, and any and all other securities on margin and to maintain a margin account, intending hereby to authorize the Trustee to act in such manner as it shall believe to be for the best interest of the trust estate, regarding it as a whole, even though particular investments otherwise might not be proper.

Section 5. To cause the securities or other property (other than assessable securities) which may comprise the trust estate or any part thereof to be registered in its name as trustee hereunder or in its own name, or in the name of its nominee without disclosing the trust, or (in the case of securities) to take and keep the same unregistered and to retain them or any part of them in such manner that they will pass by delivery; but no such registration or holding by the Trustee shall relieve it of liability for the safe custody and proper disposition of such trust property in accordance with the terms and provisions hereof.

Section 6. To vote any corporate stock belonging to the trust estate through its officers or by proxy, with or without power of substitution, and to execute proxies to one or more nominees, provided, however, that if any bank shall be acting as the Executor-Trustee of my estate and if any of the stock held in my estate shall include common stock of the same bank, then said stock must be voted in such manner as the then current income beneficiary or beneficiaries, as the case may be, shall direct.

Section 7. To reduce the interest rate on any mortgage constituting a part of the trust estate.

Section 8. To consent to the modification or release of any guaranty of any mortgage which it holds in the trust estate or in which it has a partial interest.

Section 9. To determine what expenses, costs, taxes and charges of all kinds shall be charged against income and what against principal, and its decision with respect thereto shall be conclusive upon all parties.

Section 10. To treat as principal or as income or partly as one and partly the other, as to it shall seem best, all realized appreciation in the value of stocks and bonds, securities or other property forming a part of the trust estate, resulting from the sale or other disposition thereof, and its decision with respect thereto shall be conclusive upon all parties.

Section 11. To determine whether premiums on investments shall be charged against principal or income or apportioned between them and whether discounts on investments shall be credited to principal or income or apportioned between them; to establish sinking funds for purposes of amortizations already started and distribute the sinking funds between principal and income or allocate all to the one or to the other as to it shall seem best.

Section 12. To treat stock dividends, dividends payable in the stocks or bonds of another company, extraordinary cash or noncash dividends, and liquidating dividends as income or as principal or partly as one and partly the other as to the Trustee shall seem best, and its decision with respect thereto shall be conclusive upon all parties.

Section 13. To make division or distribution in money or in kind or partly in money and partly in kind, including securities, real property, and undivided interests in real or personal property, making the necessary equalizations in cash, at values to be determined by the Trustee, whose judgment as to values shall be binding and conclusive upon all parties at interest.

Section 14. To collect, receive and receipt for the rents, issues, profits, and income of the trust estate.

Section 15. To institute, prosecute, defend, compromise, settle, pay and discharge all actions for or against the estate or arising in connection with the administration thereof, including inheritance taxes, estate taxes, gift taxes and income taxes, and to give or receive appropriate receipts, releases, acquittances and discharges, and the decision and acts of the Executor or Trustee shall be binding and conclusive upon all parties at interest.

Section 16. To borrow money for the benefit of the trust estate and to secure the loan by pledge or mortgage of the trust property and to renew existing loans.

Section 17. To sell publicly or privately, for cash or on time without an order of court, upon such terms and conditions as to it shall seem best, any property, real or personal, included in the estate, and the purchaser shall not be required to see the application of the proceeds.

Section 18. To improve, manage, protect and subdivide any real estate comprising the trust estate or any part thereof; to dedicate parks, streets, highways or alleys and to vacate any subdivision or part thereof, and to resubdivide the same as often as desired; to contract to sell, to grant options to purchase; to sell on any terms, to convey either with or without consideration; to convey said premises or any part thereof to a successor or successors in trust and to grant to such successor or successors in trust all of the title, estate, powers and authorities vested in the Trustee; to donate, to dedicate, to mortgage, pledge or otherwise encumber any such property, or any part thereof; to lease any such property, or any part thereof, from time to time in possession or reversion, by leases to commence *in praesenti* or *in futuro,* and upon any terms and for any period or periods of time, not exceeding in the case of any single demise the term of 198 years, and to renew or extend leases upon any terms and for any period or periods of time, and to amend, change or modify leases and the terms and provisions thereof at any time or times hereafter, to contract to make leases and to grant options to lease and options to renew leases and options to purchase the whole or any part of the reversion and to contract respecting the manner of fixing the amount of present or future rentals; to partition or to exchange said property, or any part thereof, for other real or personal property; to grant easements or charges of any kind, to release, convey or assign any right, title or interest in or about or easement appurtenant to any property or any part thereof; and to deal with any such property, and every part thereof in all other ways and for such other considerations as it would be lawful for any person owning the same to deal with the same whether similar to or different from the ways above specified, at any time or times hereafter.

Section 19. To sell outright or to lease or grant the right to mine or drill and to remove from any real property held hereunder gas, oil, sand, gravel, rock and other minerals, irrespective of whether or not any such right is to continue longer than the duration of the trust created hereunder, and should any of the above rights be exercised, any bonus, royalties, rentals, or proceeds of sale shall be allocated to the income or principal or partly to the income and partly to the principal as may in the sole discretion of my Executor or in the discretion of my Trustee be deemed to be just and equitable.

Section 20. To execute and deliver oil, gas and other mineral leases containing such unitization or pooling agreements and other provisions as the Trustee shall think fit; to execute mineral and royalty conveyances; to purchase leases, royalties and any type of mineral interest; to execute and deliver drilling contracts and other contracts, options, and other instruments necessary or desirable in engaging actively in the oil, gas or other mining business, all of the foregoing to be done with such terms, conditions, agreements, covenants, provisions, or undertakings as the Trustee shall think fit.

Section 21. To employ and compensate, out of the principal or income of the estate as to it shall seem proper, agents, accountants, brokers, attorneys in fact, attorneys at law, tax specialists, and other assistants and advisors deemed by it to be necessary for the proper settlement or administration of the estate, and to do so without liability for any neglect, omission, misconduct, or default of any such agent or attorney provided he was selected and retained with reasonable care; provided, however, that I request but do not require that my Executor-Trustee employ in the settlement of my estate and in the administration of the trust under my will that the attorney who shall have last represented me prior to my death in matters relating to my estate.

Section 22. To exercise any power herein granted with reference to the control, management, investment, or disposition of the estate or any part thereof, either as Executor or Trustee, and without having to declare in which capacity it is acting.

Section 23. To hold and retain the principal of the trust estate undivided, if more convenient to do so, until actual division becomes necessary in order to make any distribution; to hold, manage, invest and account for the several shares or parts thereof, as a single trust estate, making the division thereof only upon the books of account by proper entries; and to allocate to each a share, a part or proportionate part of the receipts and expenses; provided, however, that no such holding shall defer the vesting in possession of any estate.

Section 24. To pay the beneficiary entitled to the next successive estate dividends declared but not paid and interest or other income accrued but not received.

Section 25. To file joint income or gift tax returns with my spouse for the periods prior to my death; and in its sole discretion to pay any part or all of the taxes, interest, or penalties for such periods and for periods for which the joint returns were filed prior to my death. Any decision made by the Executor-Trustee shall be conclusive on all persons.

Section 26. To exercise any right available under the Internal Revenue Code to elect the manner in which any partnership, corporation, or other business unit shall be taxed, and, if necessary, in order to place an election into effect or in order to preserve an election which has been made, then to sell if it so elects any partnership interest or shares of stock from the trust estate for cash or for a note to any beneficiary or beneficiaries of my estate.

Section 27. To elect to defer payment of all or any part of my estate taxes pursuant to any provision of law permitting that deferral, and to enter into any agreement necessary to defer payment of those taxes, even if doing so extends the statute of limitations, regardless of whether sufficient funds are available with which to pay those taxes when due.

Section 28. To elect to value real property in my estate at its value for the use for which it qualifies as qualified real property, and to enter into any agreement necessary to make that election.

Section 29. To exercise all of the foregoing elections and any others available under any tax law, to obtain, to the extent practicable, both the optimum reduction in my estate taxes and in the income taxes estimated to be payable by my estate, the beneficiaries, and any business in my estate, and the optimum deferral of all of those taxes, without making any adjustment between income and principal or among any interests created in this will.

Section 30. To disclaim any asset, power of appointment or other interest in property to which I am entitled at my death, or to which my estate later becomes entitled, to minimize taxes estimated to be payable by my estate or the beneficiaries.

Section 31. To disclaim or release any right or discretion granted in this will or by applicable law, if doing so would be in the best interest of my estate or the beneficiaries; to make that disclaimer or release by an acknowledged instrument filed in a court of competent jurisdiction, or in any other manner recognized by law.

Section 32. To budget the estimated annual income and expenses of the trust in such manner as to equalize so far as practicable periodical income payments to beneficiaries.

Section 33. To transfer any asset from one of the trusts under this will to any other trust under this will by purchase, sale, loan or exchange at values to be determined by the Trustee whose judgment as to value shall be binding and conclusive upon all parties at interest, and upon such terms and conditions as it shall seem advisable.

Section 34. To deduct the costs and expenses incurred in the administration of my estate either to reduce the income tax liability of my estate or the federal estate tax liability thereof so that, in the judgment of my Executor-Trustee, the smallest combined federal estate tax and federal income tax shall be paid by my estate and the beneficiaries thereof without regard to the effect of such action upon the comparative values of the trusts created hereunder, and my Executor-Trustee shall not be required to make any compensating adjustments in either the income or principal of the several trusts created hereunder.

Section 35. To take any action and to make any election to minimize the tax liabilities of my estate, any trust created hereunder, and respective beneficiaries thereof. This power shall include but shall not be limited to the power to select assets to be sold by my estate and to be distributed to various beneficiaries in a manner which will minimize the total income tax of the estate and the various beneficiaries of my estate, but no beneficiary of my estate shall have the right to challenge the selection of assets chosen for distribution to a particular beneficiary.

Section 36. To exercise any and all of the rights, powers, and discretions granted by this will without giving prior notice to any person and without first obtaining an order of court therefor.

Section 37. To do all other acts which, in its judgment, may be necessary or appropriate for the proper and advantageous management, investment and distribution of my estate.

ARTICLE XII. Notwithstanding any provision of this will here-inbefore made, my Executor may distribute the income earned by my estate during administration thereof in the manner hereinafter set forth, provided, however, that the duration of this power shall be for the lesser of the two following periods: (1) From the date of my death until the final audit of the United States Estate Tax Return filed in my estate, or (2) from the date of my death until the end of the fourth fiscal year after the date of my death, with the first of the four fiscal years to be deemed to commence upon the first day of the month in which my death shall occur:

First, my Executor shall pay to my widow any additional income of my estate which in my Executor's discretion may be needed by her for her comfortable maintenance and support.

Finally, all the remaining income of my estate may be either (1) accumulated in whole or in part and added to the principal of my estate, or (2) distributed in whole or in part to all or any of the current income beneficiaries of the Family Trusts created by this will, and my Executor shall not be under a duty to make a ratable distribution thereof, but instead shall have the right to make distributions according to the respective needs of the current income beneficiaries according to my Executor's discretion.

The discretionary rights granted to my Executor shall not be subject to modification or interpretation by any court for any cause whatsoever.

The word "income" as hereinbefore used shall be that sum equal to taxable income as computed by my Executor for United States income tax purposes, plus income, if any, upon tax free municipals, and this definition shall not be modified as a result of any audit made by the Internal Revenue Service of any fiduciary income tax return filed in my estate.

I, John Doe, residing in Any Town, Any State, being now in good health of body and mind and not acting under duress, menace, fraud or undue influence of any person whatsoever, do make, publish and declare this my last will and testament, and do hereby expressly revoke all other and former wills and codicils to will heretofore made by me.

IN WITNESS WHEREOF, I have hereunto set my hand this _____ day of _____, 19____.

A LIVING REVOCABLE TRUST

The parties to this trust agreement are John Doe, donor, and Charles Doe, trustee, both of Any Town, Any County, Any State, WITNESSETH:

ARTICLE I

A. The donor has executed this trust agreement as a part of a comprehensive plan for the comfort and support of his wife and children in the manner hereinafter provided.

B. The donor has deposited with the trustee certain policies of insurance of the donor's life which are described in Schedule A attached hereto.

C. From time to time further property, including policies of life insurance, may be deposited with the trustee hereunder; and the donor intends to direct by the provisions of his last will that the residue of his probate estate shall pass to the trustee of this trust for administration hereunder after the donor's death.

ARTICLE II

A. The original trustee acknowledges receipt of the insurance policies listed in the schedule annexed hereto.

B. The trustee and his successor in office will hold, manage, invest and reinvest all property described in the schedule annexed and all property hereinafter deposited by the donor during his lifetime and accepted by the trustee, and all of the proceeds of said property, upon the uses and for the purposes hereinafter set forth.

C. The acting trustee will accept and administer hereunder whatever part of the donor's probate estate is to be paid to the trustee hereunder to be so administered.

D. The original trustee and its successor or successors will use its best efforts to collect when due and thereafter will administer in accordance with the terms hereof the proceeds of all policies of insurance made payable to the trustee hereunder. Neither the trustee nor any successor shall have any responsibility, however, except as above specified as to such policies, nor as to the premiums thereof nor the interest on any loan thereon; and the insurance companies which shall have issued such policies shall have no responsibility in the premises other than to pay the proceeds of the said policies when they shall become due and payable to the trustee.

E. The trustee shall not be required to make an accounting or to file any settlement with any court unless requested by a current income beneficiary of the trust. Upon the request of any current income beneficiary, the trustee shall file a settlement with a court of competent jurisdiction. Within four months after the close of each fiscal year of the trust, the trustee will render a written account of the administration of the trust to the current income beneficiaries of the trust. The written approval of any such accounting by a majority of all current income beneficiaries (the parent, guardian or conservator acting on behalf of any beneficiary who is a minor or otherwise incompetent) shall be final and binding as to all matters stated in said account as shown thereby upon all persons (whether or not in being) who are then or thereafter may become eligible to share in either the principal or the income of said trust estate. The failure of any beneficiary to object in writing to the trustee to such an account within sixty (60) days after the receipt of the same shall be final and binding to the same extent as if the written assent were given as hereinbefore provided.

F. Upon written request by the donor, the trustee will assent to or join in the execution of any instrument presented to it by the donor and designed to enable the donor to avail himself of any of the rights reserved to him by the provisions of Article IV of this instrument.

ARTICLE III

The donor agrees with the trustee that upon the request of the trustee he will execute and deliver to the trustee such further instrument, or instruments, as such trustee may hereafter deem necessary or convenient to vest the title of the trust assets in the trustee or to evidence the legal title of the trustee thereto.

ARTICLE IV

A. During his life (except during any period of adjudicated incompetency) the donor shall have the full right to be exercised from time to time by a writing or writings, signed and acknowledged by him to be effective when delivered to the trustee hereunder:

1. To revoke this instrument entirely and to receive from the trustee all of the trust property remaining after making payment or provision for payment of all expenses connected with the administration of this trust to the date of revocation.
2. From time to time to alter or amend this instrument in any and every particular.
3. From time to time to change the identity or number, or both, of the trustees hereunder.
4. From time to time to withdraw from the operation of this trust any part or all of the trust property.

B. With respect to all policies of insurance at any time deposited hereunder by the donor and made subject to the terms of this trust, he reserves full right and authority, to be exercised by him in the manner and during the periods hereinabove in Section A of this Article IV specified:

1. To sell, assign or hypothecate any or all of said policies.
2. To exercise any option or privilege granted by said policies, including the right to change the beneficiaries of any policy.
3. To borrow any sum from the insurer or any individual, partnership, corporation or association.
4. To receive all payments, dividends, surrender values, benefits or privileges of any kind which may accrue on account of said policies.
5. To freely inspect and to withdraw from this instrument any or all of said policies.

If, because of illness, adjudicated incompetency, or for any other reason the donor shall be incapable of managing his affairs, then during all such periods the trustee may exercise one or more or all of the rights hereinabove in this Section B of Article IV enumerated, and may make use of any part or all of the income or principal of the trust property for the purpose of maintaining said policies of insurance or all or any of them in full force and good standing, or alternatively, may surrender one or more of said policies and convert the same into cash.

C. During the life of the donor (except during any period of his adjudicated incompetency) the trustee shall pay over to him or to his written order whatever part or parts or all of the income and of the principal of the trust fund he shall from time to time and in writing direct.

If the donor shall, because of prolonged illness, or for any other reason be incapable of managing his affairs, then during such periods the trustee may use, apply or expend for his direct or indirect benefit, or for the direct or indirect benefit of his wife, or for the direct or indirect benefit of one or more of his living children or for the direct or indirect benefit of one or more of said persons, whatever part, or parts, or all of the income and principal, or both, of the trust fund the said trustee shall think best.

During all periods of the donor's adjudicated incompetency, if any, the trustee shall have and exercise all of said powers of payment, use, application and expenditure of income and principal hereinabove described.

D. Neither the committee nor the guardian of the donor nor any other person other than the donor himself, except as otherwise herein provided, may exercise any of the rights reserved to the donor by the provisions of this Article IV.

ARTICLE V

The trustee shall hold all of the property in this trust for a period no longer than the life of the donor's wife and his descendants living on the date of his death and twenty years and eleven months thereafter upon and for the following uses and purposes:

A. The property in this trust shall be deemed to consist of all of the property originally in this trust and all of the property received from any other source, and the trustee shall divide on a *per stirpes* basis the property in this trust as thus calculated into as many equal shares as the donor shall have children living ten months after his death and children dead with issue surviving ten months after his death, and shall set up a separate trust for each child then living and one for the issue as a group of each deceased child with each share being known as a "Child's Trust," (for example, John Doe, Jr. Trust, Joseph Doe Trust, and Susan Doe Trust), and with the shares as a whole being identified as the "Children's Trust." The shares of this trust may be held and administered together with the trustee being under a duty only to make a separate accounting for and a separate income tax return for each Child's Trust.

B. The trustee out of the Children's Trust charging an equal portion to each Child's Trust shall pay to the donor's wife that portion of the income and principal thereof necessary to provide for the donor's wife according to the standard of living that she is enjoying at the date of the donor's death provided, however, that the trustee in its discretion shall take into consideration the individual estate of the donor's wife and any and all other sources of income and support which the donor's wife may from time to time have.

C. If in any year all or any part of the income of the Children's Trust created by this section shall not be paid to the donor's wife, such income may be accumulated insofar as it may be lawfully accumulated and added to the principal of the Children's Trust created by this section or, alternatively, such income may be distributed in the manner provided by subsequent subsections of this section.

D. Provided that a sufficient reserve of principal can be and is maintained for discharge of the benefits provided for the donor's wife, the trustee out of the Children's Trust, charging an equal portion to each Child's Trust, shall pay each of the donor's children income and principal sufficient for the maintenance and education of that child until that child has reached the age of twenty-five years.

E. Provided that only a sufficient reserve of principal can be and is maintained for discharge of the benefits provided for the donor's wife, the trustee may pay each of the donor's children out of that Child's Trust quarterly or monthly that part of the income and principal of that Child's Trust necessary to supplement his or her earnings and for the purpose of providing adequately for his or her maintenance and support. The trustee out of a Child's Trust may also advance a portion of the principal thereof to the beneficiary of that trust for the purpose of purchasing a home, or alternatively, the trustee may purchase a home as trustee for the use and benefit of that child, with the purchase to be made out of the principal of that Child's Trust and with the title to be held by the trustee until such time as the trustee deems it wise to place title in the name of the child. The trustee out of a Child's Trust may lend a portion of the principal thereof to the beneficiary of that trust for any purpose deemed sufficient by the trustee, with such loan, if any, to be made upon such terms and with such security, if any, as the trustee may require.

F. The trustee upon receiving a written direction from the wife of the donor shall be under a duty to distribute out of a Child's Trust to the beneficiary of that trust that portion of the income and principal thereof which the donor's wife shall direct to be distributed and such direction shall be honored from time to time as received by the trustee from the donor's wife.

G. Upon the death of the donor's wife, the trustee shall pay to each child, at such time or times and in such amounts as the trustee in its unlimited discretion shall deem such distribution to be in the best interest of said child, the income and principal of that Child's Trust. The power granted to the trustee to make and also to defer making a distribution, various partial distributions, and a final distribution of the principal of each Child's Trust shall not be subject to modification or interpretation by any court but shall be deemed as broadly discretionary as the power that the donor would possess if living. Inasmuch as the needs of the donor's children and their respective abilities to care for property shall differ, the trustee is not only authorized but expected to follow, if advisable, a different pattern of distribution for each child.

H. Absolute power is granted the trustee not only to relieve it from seeking judicial instruction, but also to the extent that the trustee deems it to be prudent to make determinations freely in favor of liberal distributions to current income beneficiaries. In each instance the rights of all subsequent beneficiaries shall be subordinate, but the trustee shall not be answerable to any of the lifetime beneficiaries nor to any subsequent beneficiary for anything done or omitted in favor of a current income beneficiary; but no current income beneficiary shall have the right to compel any such favorable treatment.

I. If any of the children of the donor die before this trust terminates leaving widow, widower, descendants, spouses of descendants or widow or widower of deceased descendants living at the date of said deceased child's death, the trustee shall pay his or her share of the income and principal to his widow or her widower and/or to such of his or her descendants, spouses of descendants and widow or widower of deceased descendants as said deceased child shall by will appoint, provided, however, that the donor's daughter, Susan Doe, shall not have the right to appoint to any husband that she might have anything other than an estate for his life or until his remarriage whichever shall sooner occur, and in the event of any such appointment, the donor's trustee may invade the principal of the donor's estate for the benefit of the descendants of the donor's daughter, Susan Doe, without reference to the fact that such invasion of principal will diminish the life estate benefits.

J. If any child of the donor having a power of appointment under the preceding provision does not appoint his or her share of this trust by will, or if any attempted appointment shall be invalid, the trustee shall pay and distribute his or her share of this trust to his or her children *per stirpes.*

K. If any of the children of the donor die before this trust terminates without leaving descendants living at the date of said deceased child's death and without making a valid exercise of the power of appointment provided for, the trustee shall pay his or her share of the income and of the principal of this trust equally to the other children of the donor *per stirpes.*

L.   If, pursuant to this agreement, any person other than a child of the donor shall become entitled to a portion of this trust as a beneficiary thereof, such share shall become and be impressed with a trust and held in trust by the trustee until that particular minor attains the age of twenty-five years and the trustee shall spend for each person under the age of twenty-five years as much of the income and principal of that trust as is necessary for that person's education, maintenance, and support until that person is twenty-five years of age, whereupon the trustee shall pay to that beneficiary the principal and any undistributed income of his or her trust.

M.   If at any time or from time to time any beneficiaries hereunder shall be under twenty-five years of age, the trustee is to make payments in its sole discretion in any one or more of the following ways: (1) directly to such beneficiary, (2) directly in payment of the expense of support, maintenance, education and welfare of such beneficiary, (3) to the legal or natural guardian of such beneficiary, (4) or to any relative or guardian of the person of such beneficiary who shall have custody and care of the person of such beneficiary; except, however, as and to the extent that such distribution shall be herein otherwise expressly directed. The trustee shall not be obliged to see to the application of the funds so paid, but the receipt of such payee shall be full acquittance to the trustee, and all such distributions may be without the intervention of any guardian or any court, provided, however, that the trustee in its discretion may require an accounting and take such steps as it may deem requisite to assure and enforce the due application of such money to the purposes for which it is intended.

N.   With respect to the establishment and administration of each trust above described, the donor declares that the trustee shall have full power and authority to allocate property to each trust either in cash or in kind or partly in cash and partly in kind, and the action of the trustee in this respect, particularly with respect to the value of any such property, shall be binding on all persons if made reasonably and in good faith.

O.   The trustee without the advice, consent, or approval of any court and without regard to the effect of its determinations upon the beneficiaries shall have the right in its capacity as executor under the donor's will or as trustee under this trust agreement to value assets and to elect whether deductions shall be claimed on the estate tax return or on income tax returns. The donor requests, but does not require, that determinations be made by the executor or by the trustee for the purpose of minimizing the total of combined estate, inheritance and income taxes upon the donor's estate and the beneficiaries thereof.

ARTICLE VI

This trust shall not be permitted to fail for want of a trustee. In the event of the default, death, disqualification, resignation or removal of the original trustee, then the donor appoints George Doe of Any Town, Any State, as successor trustee and in the event of the default, death, disqualification, resignation or removal of George Doe as successor trustee, the donor appoints William Doe of Any Town, Any State, as successor trustee. In the event of the default, death, disqualification, resignation or removal of William Doe as successor trustee, then the donor requests the appointment of that successor trustee nominated by the donor's wife whether the nomination be made by deed or will. In exercising this power of appointment, the donor's wife may appoint either an individual or a corporation and may make the appointment so that the appointee shall be relieved from the requirement of giving bond or required to give bond. If for any reason the donor's wife shall fail to exercise the power hereby granted or if any attempt by her to exercise this power shall be invalid and also in the event of the death, default, disqualification, resignation or removal of her appointee, the donor appoints the Any Town National Bank of Any Town, Any State, trustee of the donor's estate. It shall not be necessary for any trustee designated herein to be appointed by any court or to give bond before any court although it shall have the right to seek such recognition of its fiduciary capacity if it so desires. Neither the original trustee nor any successor trustee nominated herein shall be required to give bond as such, and any corporate trustee whether designated by this trust instrument or appointed by a court shall not be required to do any more than to pledge its corporate effects to secure the bond executed by it.

Notwithstanding the other provisions of this Article, if either of the donor's sons shall at any time be acting as trustee, then the acting trustee shall not have the power to distribute to himself or to themselves individually any portion of the principal of his trust excepting only that part thereof needful or desirable for the respective beneficiary's comfortable support and maintenance including medical, surgical, hospital, or other institutional care so that the beneficiary shall receive income and only that part of the principal, if any is necessary, that may be sufficient to maintain his station in life and the standard of living that he is enjoying on the date of the donor's death.

ARTICLE VII

Neither the original trustee nor any successor trustee shall be required to qualify as such before any court, but shall assume and hold office solely by reason of the authority contained in this trust agreement. Any trustee at any time serving hereunder may resign as trustee by delivering to the successor trustee an instrument in writing containing such resignation.

ARTICLE VIII

Each trust created hereunder shall in any event terminate twenty years and eleven months after the death of the last survivor of such of the beneficiaries hereunder as shall be living at the time of the execution of this agreement, and thereafter the property held in trust shall be discharged of trust and distributed to the persons then entitled to the income and principal thereof as if all classes had closed and interests vested according to the terms of this agreement on that date.

ARTICLE IX

This trust has been created under the laws of Any State and its validity, construction and administration shall be determined by the laws of that state.

ARTICLE X

The trustee and any successor trustee shall have the right, power and authority to receive either from the donor or from any other person by deed or will any other property to be added to this trust, provided, however, that the proceeds of any pension, deferred profit sharing, Keogh, or individual retirement account plan may not be utilized by the trustee either directly or indirectly to pay death taxes, funeral, or administrative expenses.

ARTICLE XI

The trustee and any successor trustee shall have all of the following powers:
[Use a complete set of powers such as appears in the preceding will.]

WITNESS the signature of the parties hereunto as of the _____ day of _____, 19_____.

_____
John Doe

_____
Charles Doe

STATE OF ANY STATE
ANY COUNTY

I, _____, a Notary Public in and for the County and State aforesaid, hereby certify that the foregoing Trust Agreement was produced before me in my said county by John Doe and Charles Doe and was by them and each of them signed and acknowledged to be their free and voluntary act and deed.

Given under my hand and notarial seal this _____ day of _____, 19_____.

My Commission will expire on the _____ day of _____, 19_____.

_____
Notary Public, Any County, Any State

A POUR-OVER WILL

I, John Doe, of Any Town, Any State, hereby make this my last will revoking every will heretofore made by me.

ARTICLE I. I appoint my wife, Mary Doe, Executrix of this will and Trustee of my estate and request that no bond be required of her as such. In the event of the death, default, disqualification, resignation or removal of my wife, I authorize my wife to appoint a successor Executor of this will and Trustee of my estate and to require, or not to require, the execution of a bond. In the event of the death, default, disqualification, resignation or removal of the appointee, I appoint my brother, Charles Doe, Executor of this will and Trustee of my estate and request that no bond be required of him as such. In the event of the death, default, disqualification, resignation or removal of my brother, I appoint the Any Town National Bank of Any Town, Any State, as Executor of this will and Trustee of my estate. The word "Executor," whenever used herein, shall be acting as such.

ARTICLE II. This will and the John Doe Living Revocable Trust hereinafter referred to shall be construed as if the two instruments constituted a single document.

ARTICLE III. I direct my Executor to pay all of my just debts and funeral expenses and to have a monument or marker erected at my grave and to pay out of my residuary estate all estate, inheritance, transfer and succession taxes payable by my estate or payable on the legacies given herein, and my Executor shall make no claims against any person receiving any money or property including the proceeds of insurance policies includable in my gross estate for death tax purposes on account of such taxes being assessed because of such money or property.

ARTICLE IV. I hereby declare that all of the household and homestead furniture and furnishings of every kind of character, including (but without being limited to) furniture, rugs, silver, chinaware, linens, paintings and all other similar articles which have been utilized by my wife and me in our home belong to and are the exclusive property of my wife.

ARTICLE V. I bequeath all of my personal letters, jewelry, automobiles, personal effects and clothing to my wife if she be living on the date of my death, but if she predecease me, then to my children equally *per stirpes*.

ARTICLE VI. Certain of my life insurance policies may be made payable to my testamentary trustee, thereby exempting these proceeds from Any State Inheritance Taxes. My Trustee may lend all or any portion of these life insurance proceeds with or without interest to my Executor.

ARTICLE VII. If there is no sufficient evidence as to the order of our deaths, my wife shall be presumed to have survived me and this will shall be construed upon that assumption and basis.

ARTICLE VIII. I specifically refrain from exercising any power of appointment which I may have under any will, contract, trust agreement, profit sharing agreement or otherwise, and I devise and bequeath all of my other property, real, personal or mixed, in which I have or I or my estate shall acquire any interest, present or future, vested or contingent, and excluding only interests which I have a right to appoint, to the acting Trustee under a certain instrument of living revocable trust heretofore executed by me on _____, and entitled "John Doe Living Revocable Trust" to be held and administered by the Trustee in accordance with the terms thereof as stated in said instrument of living revocable trust as originally executed but as from time to time hereinafter amended.

ARTICLE IX. If for any reason said John Doe Living Revocable Trust shall not be in existence at the time of my death, or if for any reason a court of competent jurisdiction shall declare this testamentary transfer to the Trustee of said living revocable trust to be invalid, then I hereby declare that the estate disposed of by this will shall be held, managed, invested and reinvested in exactly the manner described in the said instrument of living revocable trust for the period beginning with the date of my death, giving effect to all the then existing amendments to said trust if it shall be legal so to do, but, in any event, giving effect to said trust as now in effect by the same Trustee and the same successor Trustee therein named and defined who are to serve hereunder without the necessity of providing sureties on their bonds and for that purpose I do hereby incorporate that same instrument of living revocable trust by reference into this my last will. I also declare that said living revocable trust was signed not only before a notary public but before two witnesses before whom I executed said living revocable trust as if it constituted also a last will and testament so that, in effect, this instrument can be construed as a codicil to said John Doe Living Revocable Trust.

ARTICLE X. I empower my Executor and any successor Executor, my Trustee and any successor Trustee to have and enjoy all of the powers granted to my Trustee under the John Doe Living Revocable Trust and in addition thereto but without limitation thereon, the following express powers:

Section 1. To allot, assign, borrow, care for, collect, contract with respect to, convey, convert, deal with, dispose of, enter into, exchange, hold, improve, insure, invest, lease, manage, mortgage, grant and exercise options with respect to, take possession of, pledge, protect, receive, release, repair, sell, sue for, and in general to do any and every act and thing and to enter into and carry out any and every agreement with respect to my estate or any part thereof as the Executor would have the right to do if he or it were the individual owner thereof, and as may be deemed by my Executor to be in the best interest of the beneficiaries of my estate; and this grant of power shall be construed to embrace specifically all of the powers granted to my Trustee in said John Doe Living Revocable Trust, and shall not be limited in any way by the grant of specific powers hereinafter made.

Section 2. To file joint income or gift tax returns with my wife for the period prior to my death and, in her sole discretion, to pay any part or all of the taxes, interest or penalties for such periods and for the periods for which joint returns were filed prior to my death, with any decision made being conclusive on all persons.

Section 3. To make sales and to make and receive loans to and from said John Doe Living Revocable Trust, even though the person serving as Trustee under said trust shall be the same as the fiduciary under this will.

Section 4. To make any election under the Internal Revenue Code requisite to enable the earnings of a corporation to be taxed as a partnership, or, alternatively, the earnings of a partnership to be taxed as a corporation, and my Executor is specifically directed to review this question and take any action requisite in connection therewith within thirty (30) days after my death.

ARTICLE XI. My Executor shall not be required to file an inventory or appraisal with any court or to make any settlement, final, partial or otherwise, with any court. In lieu thereof, within four months after the close of each fiscal year of my estate, the Executor shall render a written account of the administration thereof to the current income beneficiaries thereof. The written approval of such accounting by a majority of all current income beneficiaries (the parent, guardian, or conservator acting on behalf of any beneficiary who is a minor or otherwise incompetent) shall be final and binding as to all matters stated in said account or as shown thereby upon all persons (whether or not in being) who are then or thereafter may become eligible to share in either the principal or the income of my estate. The failure of any beneficiary to object in writing to the acting fiduciary to such an account within sixty (60) days after receipt of the same shall be final and binding to the same extent as if the written assent were given as hereinbefore provided.

ARTICLE XII. Notwithstanding any provision of this will or of the John Doe Living Revocable Trust, all of the property of my estate shall be finally distributed not later than twenty years and eleven months after the date of death of the last survivor of the group composed of my wife and my descendants living on the date of my death, and at the expiration of such period if any part of my estate remains undistributed, the same shall immediately vest in and be distributed to the persons then entitled to receive the income from the trust estate in the proportions to which they are so entitled.

I, John Doe, residing in Any Town, Any County, and Any State, being now in good health of body and mind and not acting under duress, menace, fraud or undue influence of any person whatsoever, do make, publish and declare this my last will and testament, and do hereby revoke all other and former wills and codicils to wills heretofore made by me.

IN WITNESS WHEREOF, I have hereto set my hand this _____
day of _____, 19____.

_____

The foregoing instrument, consisting of this and _____ preceding
pages, was, at the date hereof, signed, published and declared by
John Doe to be his last will and testament in the presence of us, the
undersigned, who, at his request, and in his sight and presence, and
in the sight and presence of each other, have hereunto subscribed
our names as witnesses thereto, having also together seen the said
testator's name written by him at the conclusion of the will on
page _____.

_____ residing at _____

_____ residing at _____

_____ residing at _____

A TYPICAL SHORT WILL
FOR A MAN WITH A WIFE,
ADULT CHILDREN,
AND A SMALL ESTATE

I, John Doe, of Any Town, Any State, hereby make this my last will revoking every will heretofore made by me.

ARTICLE I. I appoint my wife, Mary Doe, Executrix of this will and request that no bond be required of her as such. In the event of the death, default, disqualification, resignation or removal of my wife, I appoint my brother, Charles Doe, Executor of this will and request that no bond be required of him as such. In the event of the death, default, disqualification, resignation or removal of my brother, I appoint the Any Town National Bank of Any Town, Any State, as Executor of this will. The word "Executor," whenever used herein, shall be deemed to refer to my Executor or to my Executrix, whichever shall be acting as such.

ARTICLE II. I devise and bequeath my entire estate to my Executor to be distributed by him to my wife, if living, but if she predecease me, to my children equally *per stirpes*.

ARTICLE III. I empower my Executor, and any successor Executor to allot, assign, care for, collect, contract with respect to, convey, convert, deal with, dispose of, enter into, exchange, hold, improve, insure, invest, lease, manage, mortgage, grant and exercise options with respect to, take possession of, pledge, protect, receive,

139

release, repair, sell, sue for, and in general, to do any and every act and thing and to enter into and carry out any agreement with respect to my estate or any part thereof as the Executor would have the right to do if it were the individual owner thereof and as it may deem in the best interest of the beneficiaries of my estate.

I, John Doe, residing in Any Town, Any State, being now in good health of body and mind and not acting under duress, menace, fraud or undue influence of any person whatsoever, do make, publish and declare this my last will and testament, and do hereby expressly revoke all other and former wills and codicils to wills heretofore made by me.

IN WITNESS WHEREOF, I have hereunto set my hand this _____ day of _____, 19____.

_____

The foregoing instrument, consisting of this and _____ preceding pages, was, at the date hereof, signed, published and declared by John Doe to be his last will and testament in the presence of us, the undersigned, who at his request and in his sight and presence, and in the sight and presence of each other, have hereunto subscribed our names as witnesses thereto, having also together seen the said testator's name written by him at the conclusion of the will on page _____.

_____ residing at _____

_____ residing at _____

_____ residing at _____

ESTATE AND GIFT TAX TABLE

If the taxable estate is:	The tax shall be:
Not over $10,000	18% of such amount
Over $10,000 but not over $20,000	$1,800, plus 20% of excess over $10,000
Over $20,000 but not over $40,000	$3,800, plus 22% of excess over $20,000
Over $40,000 but not over $60,000	$8,200, plus 24% of excess over $40,000
Over $60,000 but not over $80,000	$13,000, plus 26% of excess over $60,000
Over $80,000 but not over $100,000	$18,200, plus 28% of excess over $80,000
Over $100,000 but not over $150,000	$23,800, plus 30% of excess over $100,000
Over $150,000 but not over $250,000	$38,800, plus 32% of excess over $150,000
Over $250,000 but not over $500,000	$70,800, plus 34% of excess over $250,000
Over $500,000 but not over $750,000	$155,800, plus 37% of excess over $500,000
Over $750,000 but not over $1,000,000	$248,300, plus 39% of excess over $750,000
Over $1,000,000 but not over $1,250,000	$345,800, plus 41% of excess over $1,000,000
Over $1,250,000 but not over $1,500,000	$448,300, plus 43% of excess over $1,250,000
Over $1,500,000 but not over $2,000,000	$555,800, plus 45% of excess over $1,500,000
Over $2,000,000 but not over $2,500,000	$780,800, plus 49% of excess over $2,000,000
Over $2,500,000 but not over $3,000,000	$1,025,800, plus 53% of excess over $2,500,000
Over $3,000,000 but not over $3,500,000	$1,290,800, plus 57% of excess over $3,000,000
Over $3,500,000 but not over $4,000,000	$1,575,800, plus 61% of excess over $3,500,000
Over $4,000,000 but not over $4,500,000	$1,880,800, plus 65% of excess over $4,000,000
Over $4,500,000 but not over $5,000,000	$2,205,800, plus 69% of excess over $4,500,000
Over $5,000,000	$2,550,800, plus 70% of excess over $5,000,000

Note: Subject to the maximum tax rates set forth on page 142.

Under the Economic Recovery Tax Act of 1981 the maximum tax rate on estates and gifts is reduced as follows:

Year	Maximum rate
1982	65 percent
1983	60 percent
1984	55 percent
1985	50 percent

After annual exclusions and after gifts to the spouse which may also be excluded, both gift taxes and estate taxes are to be computed from the foregoing table and from the resultant tax, the following unified tax credits are to be deducted:

Year beginning	Unified tax credit	Exemption equivalent
1982	62,800	225,000
1983	79,300	275,000
1984	96,300	325,000
1985	121,800	400,000
1986	155,800	500,000
1987	192,800	600,000